Speak Basic

Spanish

...In No Time

Larry C. Rios

que

800 East 96th Street,
Indianapolis, Indiana 46290

Speak Basic Spanish In No Time

International Standard Book Number: 0-7897-3223-8

Library of Congress Catalog Card Number: 2004107642

Printed in the United States of America

First Printing: October 2004
Reprinted with corrections July 2005

09 10 11 12   9 8 7 6

Trademarks

All terms mentioned in this book that are known to be trademarks or service marks have been appropriately capitalized. Que Publishing cannot attest to the accuracy of this information. Use of a term in this book should not be regarded as affecting the validity of any trademark or service mark.

Warning and Disclaimer

Every effort has been made to make this book as complete and as accurate as possible, but no warranty or fitness is implied. The information provided is on an "as is" basis. The author and the publisher shall have neither liability nor responsibility to any person or entity with respect to any loss or damages arising from the information contained in this book.

Bulk Sales

Que Publishing offers excellent discounts on this book when ordered in quantity for bulk purchases or special sales. For more information, please contact

U.S. Corporate and Government Sales
1-800-382-3419
corpsales@pearsontechgroup.com

For sales outside of the U.S., please contact

International Sales
international@pearsoned.com

Executive Editor
Candace Hall

Development Editor
Lorna Gentry

Managing Editor
Charlotte Clapp

Project Editor
Andrew Beaster

Production Editor
Benjamin Berg

Proofreader
Paula Lowell

Indexer
Julie Bess

Technical Editor
Mindy Baker

Publishing Coordinator
Cindy Teeters

Multimedia Developer
Dan Scherf

Interior Designer
Anne Jones

Cover Designer
Anne Jones

Cover Illustrator
Nathan Clement, Stickman Studio

Page Layout
Susan Geiselman

Contents at a Glance

Table of Contents

About the Author

Larry C. Rios has always had a passion for writing, but his greater passion has always been to share his knowledge of the Spanish language. After receiving a degree in accounting from New Mexico State University, he spent the first half of his career writing. He wrote functional specifications that were coded by programmers, and the operating manuals for accounting systems he designed. Upon retirement from federal service, as a budget officer, he pursued his passion by starting an English-to-Spanish translation service on the Internet in 1999. He provides English-to-Spanish and Spanish-to-English translation with audio at www.sayitinspanish.com.

Dedication

This book is dedicated to my loving wife, Esther, and two sons, Larry and Randy, for their love and support.

Acknowledgements

I get a lot of satisfaction when I am able to help someone who is trying to learn to speak Spanish. I could only dream about having the opportunity to do it at this level.

I owe special thanks to Candace Hall, Que executive editor, who recognized the need to provide people a simple way to learn to speak basic Spanish. She provided me an opportunity I could only dream of. Lorna Gentry's encouragement and editing made my work look good. Mindy Baker's technical editing ensured the translations were correct. The other members of the Que staff that worked on this book helped to make this book a useful tool.

We Want to Hear from You!

As the reader of this book, you are our most important critic and commentator. We value your opinion and want to know what we're doing right, what we could do better, what areas you'd like to see us publish in, and any other words of wisdom you're willing to pass our way.

As an executive editor for Que Publishing, I welcome your comments. You can email or write me directly to let me know what you did or didn't like about this book as well as what we can do to make our books better.

Please note that I cannot help you with technical problems related to the topic of this book. We do have a User Services group, however, where I will forward specific technical questions related to the book.

When you write, please be sure to include this book's title and author as well as your name, email address, and phone number. I will carefully review your comments and share them with the author and editors who worked on the book.

Email: feedback@quepublishing.com

Mail: Candace Hall
Executive Editor
Que Publishing
800 East 96th Street
Indianapolis, IN 46240 USA

For more information about this book or another Que Publishing title, visit our website at www.quepublishing.com. Type the ISBN (excluding hyphens) or the title of a book in the Search field to find the page you're looking for.

Introduction

How do you feel when you hear someone speak in a language that you do not understand? Do you try to ignore their conversation or pretend that you just don't care? Do you think they're being rude and wonder if they might be talking about you? My primary language is Spanish, and I was exposed to being the language "outsider" when my family and I lived in Honolulu, Hawaii. As I rode the elevator to our apartment on the 38th floor, I would hear people speaking in Chinese, Korean, and Japanese, and I did not understand a thing they were saying. It took me a while to get over being uncomfortable in those situations. After you read this book, you won't have to worry about being uncomfortable when you hear someone talking in Spanish. This book will teach you to speak and understand basic conversational Spanish.

Speak Basic Spanish…In No Time makes it fun and easy to learn to speak Spanish. This book is designed especially for someone who wants to learn quickly to have casual conversations in Spanish, but does not have the time to go through a voluminous textbook and absorb numerous advanced language conventions. You will not be required to master any grammatical rules, nor will you be required to read a ton of material. And, you'll learn *how* to speak as well as what to say. There are certain unique sounds in Spanish not found in the English language. This book will teach you how to generate those sounds without having to put your mouth, lips, and tongue through impossible gyrations. You will learn by hearing.

This book allows you to select the material you want to learn from the table of contents and go directly to that chapter. Many books on learning Spanish require that you learn complicated syntax and how to generate complicated Spanish sounds, without audio. In *Speak Basic Spanish…In No Time*, each chapter includes easily accessible audio files that will teach you how to speak Spanish by hearing the words in a clear, slow voice. That is how we learned to talk when we were children—by hearing others talk.

Before we move any further, though, let me define the assumptions I've made about whom you will be talking to in Spanish. There is a never-ending debate over what to call people whose native tongue is Spanish. Some of the names tossed around are Latino, Spanish, Hispanic, Hispano, Mexican, Mexican-American, Spanish-American, and Chicano. These names are derived from an individual's country of origin, ancestry, or culture. I do not plan to enter or attempt to settle the debate. I had to settle on a term that identifies a group of people based on the language they speak, and not their country of origin, ancestry, or culture. The term *Hispanic* will be used throughout this book to refer to a person whose primary language is Spanish. The translated Spanish is that which is spoken in most Latin American countries. It does not include the Castilian Spanish spoken in Spain.

note After you learn the phrases and techniques presented in this book, a Spaniard will understand your Spanish and you will understand the majority of his Spanish. You may notice, however, that his pronunciation of certain words is different. In Spain, for example, they pronounce the letters "ci" and "ce", which sound like "see" and "seh" in English, with a "th" sound. The Spanish word "gracias" pronounced "grah-see-us" in Latin American countries is pronounced "gra-thee-us" in Spain. The second thing you will notice is that a Spaniard uses "vosotros" as the plural of tú, instead of "ustedes."

Who Should Read This Book

Learn to speak basic Spanish and you will be amazed at how it will change your life. You no longer have to live in or travel to Texas, New Mexico, or California to encounter Hispanic residents, shopkeepers, and business owners. Nearly every part of the United States has seen a dramatic increase in the Hispanic population. If you can't speak Spanish, you are missing valuable opportunities to interact with this important segment of our nation's life and culture.

You may simply want to learn enough Spanish to carry on a casual conversation with non—English-speaking Hispanics about family, jobs, schools, weather, food, clothes, pets, or leisure activity. This alone is an experience that will enrich your life. You will have the confidence to enter a Hispanic restaurant or other business and know what you are ordering or purchasing. If you require assistance at some business from Hispanic employees that do not speak English you will be able to convey your needs to them.

If you are in business, this book will provide you with the ability to communicate with Hispanics in Spanish. You will be able to market your products to Hispanics, in Spanish, in person, and through any advertising medium. And, if you are planning a visit to Spain or other Spanish-speaking regions of the world, this book will prepare you for making reservations, eating out, and holding basic, casual conversations with the local residents.

How to Use This Book

This book provides an extensive list of words and sentences, with audio, arranged by topic. Some expressions, such as greetings, are repeated in a couple of chapters. This helps to make the conversation presented in that chapter more complete. You don't need to read this book from cover-to-cover. You can browse through the table of contents and find the chapter that contains the topic you want learn and go directly to that chapter. Cross-references guide you to related information elsewhere in the book, so you can take advantage of techniques and examples that build upon each other. Each chapter identifies the audio file that contains the related translations. If you learn the majority of the translated material within a chapter you will be able to converse about the subjects covered in that chapter.

What's in the Book?

Part I, "Quick Guide to the Basics," takes you quickly through the basics of Spanish grammar and pronunciation. The only chapter of this book that contains material resembling instruction is Chapter 1, "The Rules—Short and Sweet." It provides a few basic rules on grammar, explains noun and adjective gender, and introduces you to the Spanish accent. It is not really necessary to learn the material in that chapter to learn to speak Spanish, but it will help you understand how a combination of letters, with an accent thrown in here and there, can sound so different in English and Spanish. If you read the material on the effect of accents on pronunciation, you will be able to read and pronounce written Spanish words not included in this book.

Chapter 2, "Letters, Numbers, Dates, and Dollars," gives you a quick, useful guide to using the alphabet, numbers, and units of measurement in Spanish.

Part II of this book is titled "Talking about Your Daily Life." In this part of the book, you learn how to conduct simple conversations about the people, places, things, and events that make up your world. Imagine the many directions a conversation can take if you greet someone with the simple question, "How are you?" The response may be a plain "I'm fine," or the reply may lead you into a discussion of health issues; problems at home, the house, at work; or a bad meal at the restaurant.

From that first "getting to know you" conversation to talks about your family members, home, job, friends, and hobbies, in Part II of this book you learn basic terms and phrases for talking about your life in Spanish. You learn how to describe your clothes and discuss interests such as television programs and pets, as well as how to hire home repair workers and rent a house or apartment. You learn how to talk with others about your job, school, sports, and other personal interests. This part also describes important terms and phrases you'll use when shopping, cooking, going to the doctor, eating out, and other common daily activities.

In Part III, "Special Situations," you learn how to participate in simple conversations about a wide variety of special situations you might encounter. You learn phrases and simple sentences you'll use when staying at a hotel, or when discussing nature, weather, seasons, and other scientific subjects. You'll also learn how to describe and discuss computers and their technologies, as well as a variety of professional topics, including sales, investments, and legal issues. You also learn how to talk about the media, politics, government, and your rights and responsibilities as a citizen. Finally, this part offers a fast-track reference to selected words, phrases, and sentences that you're almost certain to use as you begin speaking in Spanish.

Special Elements

Throughout this book, you'll find a variety of special elements, including lists, sidebars, icons, and other "extras" designed to catch your eye and call out items of special interest relevant to the nearby text. Some of these items are described here, but as you read the book, you'll quickly spot these special elements and learn how to use their information as you learn the basics of conversational Spanish.

Useful Lists

Each chapter of the book opens with an "In This Chapter" section that gives you a quick scan of what you'll do or learn within that chapter. Each chapter also includes Listen Up! lists that point you toward all of the audio files that accompany the chapter's text. *Speak Basic Spanish...In No Time* also includes a variety of bulleted and numbered lists to help you quickly learn—and remember—series of items and simple steps.

Other Special Information

In addition to traditional notes and tips, we'll call out other helpful information in easy-to-spot graphic formats, to help make *Speak Basic Spanish...In No Time* an interesting and informative guide. Watch for these helpful items:

TALKING POINTS

Throughout the book, you'll notice these sidebars, designed to bring you examples, short anecdotes, and insights into Hispanic life and culture that will make the process of learning to speak Spanish more meaningful and enjoyable for you!

Speaking of... items direct you to information elsewhere in the book or resources guide that is related to the current topic.

This icon marks especially important grammar or pronunciation guides, potential areas of confusion, or other "heads-up" information that will help you become fluent quickly and avoid common language errors.

Listen up! references direct you to the appropriate audio file for the current section.

Finally, all translated text is shown in *italics*, and this translated text is also included on the accompanying audio file.

Using the Audio Files

The audio files are maintained at http://www.quepublishing.com. Type the ISBN of the book (10-digit number listed next to the bar code on the back of your book) into the Search field. On the book's web page you'll find a More Information box listing the audio files. You can listen to the audio files online or download them onto your computer. If you download them to your computer, you can copy them to a CD and play them without having to go online. The audio file will include the English words or sentences and their translations into Spanish. You will be able to read the words and sentences in your book as you play the audio for the respective topic. A few repetitions will help you learn basic written and spoken Spanish words and their meaning in English.

All translations are presented with the English text and audio followed by the respective Spanish translated text and audio. If you initiate the conversation, your statement will be shown in English. If the Hispanic person initiates the conversation, that person's statement will be shown in English followed by the Spanish translation. This allows you to hear in English what the Hispanic person has said in Spanish.

To ensure that you hear what the Hispanic person meant to say, every effort is made to have the translated text reflect the meaning of the original statement. Literal translation does not always convey the intended meaning of a statement. For example, the literal translation of "passing the buck" results in a phrase that says, "transferring the dollar." A non-literal translation results in the more accurate translated phrase, "transferring responsibility." Every effort is made to have the target language reflect what the original language meant to convey.

What This Book Will Do for You

What do you have to gain by learning to speak Spanish? In my opinion, the most significant thing you will gain is that you will bond with some of the friendliest people on earth. Many non–English-speaking Hispanics know how to speak a little bit of English. They will not initiate a conversation because they do not know how it will be received. If, however, someone makes an effort to speak to them in their native language, they will make every effort to understand what you are trying to say to them. They will help your attempt to communicate with them by applying whatever knowledge they may have of the English language.

Secondly, if you are in some kind of business, you will be able to capitalize on a growing lucrative market. *Speak Basic Spanish...In No Time* provides you with a significant number of translated conversations that you can use to communicate with your Hispanic clients and inform them about your business. The translated material can also be used in advertising and television commercials.

You can be proud of the fact that you have taken the first step in learning a new language. You will be glad that you did.

Part 1

Quick Guide to the Basics

Audio Files

- ☐ 01a Vowels
- ☐ 01b Special characters and accents
- ☐ 01c Unique sounds
- ☐ 01d Gender of nouns and adjectives
- ☐ 01e Grammar complexities

The Rules—Short and Sweet

If you walk into any bookstore or search the Internet for books on how to read and speak Spanish, you will be amazed at how much material there is. And the instructions in most books that do not include audio are mind-boggling. There are so many rules that you must learn in order to be able to read or speak Spanish, and for every rule, there seems to be an exception. The grammar rules alone could make you decide to just hang it up and forget about learning Spanish. *Speak Basic Spanish In No Time* is different; it assumes that you are more interested in learning how to speak, rather than read, Spanish. Using the text and the audio files that accompany this book, you learn to speak by listening and repeating what you learned.

This chapter focuses on some fundamental skills in pronouncing and using the Spanish language. You learn how to pronounce vowels in Spanish, as well as the meaning of special characters used in written Spanish, and how they affect word pronunciation. You also learn how the combinations of certain letters affect pronunciation of Spanish words. This chapter also explains noun and adjective gender, and how they are reflected in the Spanish language. Finally, the chapter describes a few of the complexities of Spanish grammar, including how to match verbs with the subject and tense of any sentence.

You may be wondering why, if we intend to focus on spoken Spanish, we begin the book with a chapter that

1

In this chapter:

- ✳ Learning to pronounce vowels and letters accompanied by special characters and accents
- ✳ Pronouncing letter combinations
- ✳ Understanding the effect of gender on nouns and adjectives

lists grammar rules. Our purpose is twofold: to help you understand how certain letters and combination of letters can sound different when pronounced in English and in Spanish, and to provide you the ability to read and pronounce words not included in this book. If you plan to learn to read and speak Spanish beyond the basic conversation level, you'll make good use of the Spanish grammar rules you learn here.

As the title promises, we've kept these rules short and sweet. We don't offer lengthy textbook-style material on Spanish grammar, but we do give you some fundamental rules that will help you speak and understand Spanish in casual conversations. By reviewing these rules and referring to them periodically as you progress through this book, you'll soon be comfortable with your ability to speak Spanish with your friends and co-workers.

Pronouncing Vowels and Using Special Characters

If you learn how to pronounce the Spanish vowels correctly, you will greatly improve your ability to speak Spanish and sound like a Hispanic. In this section, you learn the correct pronunciation of vowels in Spanish. Special characters also help determine the pronunciation of Spanish words. In this section you will see how an accent (´) over a syllable in a word affects how that word is pronounced. The tilde (~) on top of the letter N creates a separate letter (Ñ). Finally, the Spanish language uses some familiar punctuation marks in ways that may be unfamiliar to you. In this section we will also describe the inverted question and exclamation marks, and how they are used in a sentence.

note Audio files 01a through 01d differ from the other audio files included in this book. In the material included within these audio files, we are trying to show you how to pronounce Spanish words using pronunciation guides. These audio files include only the Spanish pronunciation of the word being discussed. The text will include the English word in parenthesis following the Spanish word, and a phonetic spelling of the Spanish word.

Go to audio file 01a Vowels.

Pronouncing Vowels

Pronunciation is critical in learning how to speak any language. It is easy to learn how to pronounce Spanish words, because Spanish is a phonetic language. The Spanish vowel has only one sound, a short vowel sound. On the audio file that accompanies this section, you hear the following vowels pronounced in Spanish:

a	ah
e	eh

i	ee
o	oh
u	oo

In Spanish, vowel sounds generally remain the same regardless of the word they are in or the letter they are adjacent to. There are a few exceptions, which we address in the next paragraph. English vowels are much more difficult.

There is a slight change in pronunciation that may take place when Spanish vowels are adjacent to other vowels. Two vowel combinations that include an unaccented u or i are called *diphthongs*. Diphthongs are pronounced as one syllable. Strong vowels are A, E, O. Weak vowels are I and U. When a strong and a weak vowel are together, the stress falls on the strong vowel (it is the one that you hear more predominantly). Some examples are

baile (dance)	BAHY-leh
puesto (stall)	PWEHS-toh
causa (cause)	COW-sah
cuatro (four)	KWAH-troh

> **note** English vowel sounds can vary based on whether they are long or short vowels, and what letters precede or follow them. Note the different sounds of the letter A in the words *fad*, *fade*, and *father*. Note how a variety of vowel combinations can produce the sound of the long E in the following words: *see*, *sea*, *fatigue*, *grief*, *receive*, and *machine*.

In a combination of weak and weak the stress falls on the second vowel, as illustrated here:

cuidado (caution)	kwee-DAH-doh
ciudad (city)	see-oo-DAHD

When two strong vowels are combined, they are not a diphthong; instead, they are pronounced as two separate syllables. Here are a couple of examples:

real (real)	wreh-AHL
feo (ugly)	FEH-oh

If a written accent breaks the diphthong, then both vowels are pronounced as two separate syllables:

tía (aunt)	TEE-ah
día (day)	DEE-ah
estación (season)	ehs-tah-syOHN

> **tip** To help learn the Spanish pronunciation of vowels, be sure to listen to the vowel sounds as you play the various audio files in each chapter.

Using Special Characters and Accent Symbols

Special characters in written Spanish change the way certain letters are pronounced. With no special character, for example, the letter U is silent when used with *gui*, *gue*, and when it follows the letter Q:

Go to audio file 01b Special characters and accents.

guiar (guide)	gee-AHR, "gee" as in geese
guerra (war)	GUE-rah, "gue" as in guerilla
quince (fifteen)	KEEN-seh

Note that in the preceding words, the G is pronounced as a hard G. In the following examples, the letter U is marked with an umlaut (¨). The umlaut used above the *U* changes the way the G and U sound in the "gui" and "gue" combination of letters:

| *pingüino* (penguin) | peen-GOOWEE-no |
| *güero* (blond) | gooEH-roh |

A tilde over the letter N changes its sound. The *ñ* sounds like the *ni* in the English word onion.

| *año (year)* | *AH-nyoh* |
| *cañón* (canyon) | cah-nyOHN |

An inverted question mark (¡) or exclamation point (¿) at the beginning of the sentence and then a regular one at the end of the sentence identify questions and exclamations in written forms.

| *¿Estás bien? (Are you okay?)* | ¿Eh-STAHS byen? |
| *¡Cuidado!* (Careful!) ¿Kwee-DAH-doh! |

If a sentence includes both a positive statement (called a *declarative*) and a question (called an *interrogative*), only the question is enclosed by the interrogative signs:

Go to audio file 01c Unique sounds.

Estás bien, ¿verdad? (You are okay, right?)
Eh-STAHS-byen, ¿vehr-DAHD?

In Spanish, as in English, words with more than one syllable are pronounced with stress or emphasis on certain syllables. The three rules for the placement of this emphasis in Spanish are generally consistent and easy to remember:

1. If a word ends in a vowel, or the consonants N or S, you place the stress on the next-to-the-last syllable.

2. If a word ends in a consonant other than N or S, you place the stress on the last syllable.

3. If the stress is on a syllable that does not conform to the preceding rules, an accent symbol is placed over the vowel in the syllable that is to be stressed.

If you learn these simple rules you will be able to read and pronounce most Spanish words.

The following are examples of Spanish words that demonstrate each of these rules. In each of these examples, the stressed syllable is capitalized and underscored in the Spanish term.

These examples illustrate Rule 1, which states that if a word ends in a vowel, or the consonants N or S, you place the stress on the next to the last syllable:

co<u>ci</u>na (kitchen)	koh-<u>SEE</u>-nah
ca<u>mi</u>no (road)	kah-<u>MEE</u>-noh
Ellos ca<u>mi</u>nan. (They walk.)	<u>EH</u>-yohs kah-<u>MEE</u>-nahn
pantal<u>o</u>nes (pants)	pahn-tah-<u>LOHN</u>-ehs
<u>jo</u>ven (young man)	<u>HOH</u>-vehn

The following examples illustrate Rule 2, which states that if the word ends in a consonant other than N or S, you place the stress on the last syllable:

cal<u>or</u> (heat)	kah-<u>LOHR</u>
verd<u>ad</u> (truth)	vehr-<u>DAHD</u>
crist<u>al</u> (crystal)	krees-<u>TAHL</u>
compl<u>ot</u> (conspiracy)	kohm-<u>PLOHT</u>

These examples illustrate Rule 3, which states that if the stress is on a syllable that does not conform to the other two rules, an accent symbol is placed over the vowel in the syllable that is to be stressed:

él coci<u>nó</u>. (He cooked.)	Ehl koh-see-<u>NOH</u>
Ella cami<u>nó</u>. (She walked.)	<u>EH</u>-ya kah-mee-<u>NOH</u>
Lat<u>ín</u> (Latin)	Lah-<u>TEEN</u>
fil<u>ó</u>sofo (philosopher)	fee-<u>LOH</u>-soh-foh
ingl<u>és</u> (English)	een-<u>GLEHS</u>

Letters and Letter Combinations that Create Unique Spanish Sounds

The sound of consonants changes significantly when they are doubled or combined with another consonant. In this section we provide some examples of these letter combinations and their pronunciations.

Listening to the Spanish alphabet in audio file 02a Alphabet (which accompanies Chapter 2), will help you hear how the sound is altered when the consonants are doubled, or combined with other letters.

Go to audio file 01c Unique sounds.

The B and the V sound alike in Spanish, as shown here:

beber (drink)	beh-<u>BEHR</u>
escribir (write)	ehs-cree-<u>BEER</u>
pasivo (passive)	pah-<u>SEE</u>-boh
vacación (vacation)	Bah-cah-sy<u>OHN</u>

The *C* followed followed by an *E* or *I* has a soft sound that sounds like a short *S* in English (as in the word *sister*). When the C is followed by an *A*, *O*, or *U* it has the *K* sound heard in the English term *cat*. Here are some examples:

cerámico (ceramic)	sehr-<u>AH</u>-mee-koh
sidra (cider)	SEE-drah
cabeza (head)	kah-<u>BEH</u>-sah
coche (auto)	<u>KOH</u>-cheh
cuaderno (notebook)	kwah-<u>DEHR</u>-noh

The *CH* letter combination is pronounced the same as it is in the English term *chair*. Here is an example:

chabacano (apricot)	chah-bah-<u>CAH</u>-noh

The letter *G* followed by *A*, *O*, or *U* is pronounced as it is in the English word *go*. Here are some examples:

gasolina (gasoline)	gah-soh-<u>LEE</u>-nah
goma (gum)	<u>GOH</u>-mah
guante (glove)	<u>GWAHN</u>-teh

The *G* followed by *E* or *I* has a soft sound like the *H* in *Hope*.

gelatina (gelatin)	heh-lah-<u>TEE</u>-nah
gimnasio (gymnasium)	heem-<u>NAH</u>-syoh

The *H* in Spanish is always silent.

hispano (Hispanic)	ees-<u>PAH</u>-noh
helado (ice cream)	eh-<u>LAH</u>-doh

The *J* sound is like the *H* sound in English.

jabón (soap)	hah-<u>BOHN</u>
caja (box)	<u>KAH</u>-hah

The *ll* sounds like the *y* sound in English.

llamada (call)	yah-<u>MAH</u>-thah
llave (key)	<u>YAH</u>-veh
collar (necklace)	koh-YAHR

R-R-R-RUFFLES HAVE R-R-R-RIDGES

You may remember the Ruffles potato chip commercials on TV. The announcers in those ads did a good job of rolling their Rs. The "rolling" sound of *RR* is unique to Spanish—there is no sound in English similar to it. The written instruction on how to pronounce this *RR* letter combination is to "roll it," "let the tip of your tongue vibrate near your upper teeth," and to "trill it". We have used the quadruple R in the phonetic spelling of words that include the *RR*.

ferrocarril (railroad)   feh-rrrroh-cah-<u>RRRREEL</u>

carretera (road)   kah-rrrreh-<u>TEH</u>-rah

The best way to learn how to pronounce the *RR* sound is to hear it repeatedly and say it. Listen to the sound of the rolling Rs on the audio files that accompany this chapter. Then, try to repeat the following saying, which simply states that the dogs run rapidly after the train.

Rápido corren los perros, detrás del ferrocarril.

The single *R* has two sounds. The normal sound is a soft sound as in:

aire (air)	<u>AHY</u>-reh

The single *R* has the *RR* sound described above if the R is at the beginning of a word or preceded by the letters *L, O, N,* or *S.* Here are some examples:

roca (rock)	<u>ROH</u>-kah
alrededor (around)	ahl-reh-deh-<u>DOHR</u>
sonrisa (smile)	sohn-<u>REE</u>-sah
transrecibidor (transceiver)	trahns-reh-see-bee-<u>DOHR</u>

The *z* in Spanish is pronounced like a soft *S*, as in this example:

    zacate (grass)   sah-<u>KAH</u>-teh

Go to audio file 01e Grammar complexities.

Double consonants such as *TT*, *MM*, *NN*, *FF* are not used in Spanish. The letter combination *PH* does not exist in Spanish; the *F* is used instead.

Using Masculine and Feminine Nouns

In Spanish, all nouns have a gender; in other words, Spanish nouns are either masculine or feminine. The rules for determining what gender to assign a noun are varied. Although we won't include all of them in this section, we will cover some of the more basic rules.

LONERS CAN HELP

If you remember the mnemonic "LONERS," it will help you identify the masculine gender of nouns. A couple of simple rules to remember are

Most Spanish nouns that end in L-O-N-E-R-S are masculine.

Most Spanish nouns that end in a-dad-ión are feminine.

Here are some examples of Spanish nouns ending in L-O-N-E-R-S (masculine gender):

Go to audio file 01d Gender of nouns and adjectives

    canal (canal)   kah-<u>NAHL</u>
    gato (male cat)   <u>GAH</u>-toh
    buzón (mailbox)   boo-<u>SOHN</u>
    chicle (chewing gum)   <u>CHEE</u>-kleh
    calor (heat)   kah-<u>LOHR</u>
    mes (month)   mehs

The following examples of Spanish nouns ending in "a", "dad", and "ión" (*a-dad-ión*) are feminine gender:

    gata (female cat)   <u>GAH</u>-tah
    verdad (truth)   vehr-<u>DAHD</u>
    canción (song)   kahn-sy<u>OHN</u>

There are some exceptions to the rules. In the following examples, it does not matter what the gender of the subject is; the noun that identifies the profession *artista* is feminine. In these cases, the translation for the indefinite article "an," (*un* and *una*) identifies the masculine and feminine genders.

un artista (a male artist)	oon-ahr-<u>TEES</u>-tah
una artista (a female artist)	<u>OON</u>-ah-ahr-<u>TEES</u>-tah

The definite article "the" has four possible translations depending on the gender of the noun, and whether the noun is singular or plural, as shown in these examples:

El niño (The child)	Ehl <u>NEE</u>-nyoh
Los niños (The children)	Lohs <u>NEE</u>-nyohs
La niña (The child)	Lah <u>NEE</u>-nyah
Las niñas (The children)	Lahs <u>NEE</u>-nyahs

THE IMPORTANCE OF CORRECT TRANSLATION

Talking Points

Incorrect translation can produce embarrassing results. There was a story circulating on the Internet a few years back about American Airlines promoting their brand new leather seats in first class. "Fly in leather," they said. Unfortunately, when this was directly translated for the Spanish speaking market as *Vuela en cuero*, the translation came out "Fly naked."

Using Masculine and Feminine Adjectives

The adjective assumes the gender of the noun it describes, as illustrated in the examples given here. In the first example, *hombre*, a singular masculine noun, is modified by the singular adjective *pequeño*:

hombre pequeño   <u>OHM</u>-breh peh-<u>KEH</u>-nyoh
(small man)

In the second example, *mujeres*, the plural feminine noun is modified by the plural adjective *pequeñas*:

mujeres pequeñas   moo-<u>HEHR</u>-ehs peh-<u>KEH</u>-nyahs
(small women)

Adjective word endings have to agree in number (singular/plural) and gender (masculine/feminine) with the nouns they describe. In the following examples we use the color red to describe different gender and number of articles of clothing.

traje rojo (red suit)	<u>TRAH</u>-heh <u>RRRROH</u>-hoh
camisa roja (red shirt)	kah-<u>MEE</u>-sah <u>RRRROH</u>-hah
zapatos rojos (red shoes)	sah-<u>PAH</u>-tohs <u>RRRROH</u>-hohs
blusas rojas (red blouses)	<u>BLOO</u>-sahs <u>RRRROH</u>-hahs

Tackling Two Spanish Grammar Complexities

We stated at the beginning of this chapter that learning to speak Spanish is easy because it is a phonetic language. Spanish grammar, however, can be somewhat complex. Fortunately, you don't have to memorize every detail of Spanish grammar in order to learn to speak basic Spanish as taught by this book. Nevertheless, some grammar rules can be basic to conversational Spanish. In this chapter, we tackle two of these areas: using the prepositions *para* and *por*, and matching verbs with their subject and tense. You don't need to worry about memorizing these rules right now, but you can work on practicing them as you progress through the remainder of this book.

The audio file in this section includes both English and Spanish audio.

Go to audio file 01e Grammar complexities

note Understanding Spanish grammar will help you master the language and learn to communicate freely and fluently in Spanish. The information provided here gives you a foundation of understanding of the grammatical rules of the language; if you wish to learn Spanish grammar, however, you should enroll in a course that teaches Spanish.

Using the Prepositions *para* and *por*

There are two Spanish words, *para* and *por*, that are often misused because they are both the translation of the preposition "for". These two words are also the translation for other words and phrases, such as "by," and "in order to."

Use *para* when describing actions done for someone's or something's benefit, a destination, a specific time, or identifying a recipient of an action.

I bought food for my dog.	*Compré comida para mi perro.*
I went to buy food.	*Fui para comprar comida.*
The gift is for her.	*El regalo es para ella.*
They left for Chicago.	*Salieron para Chicago.*

I made it for you.	*Lo hice para usted.*
He works for her.	*él trabaja para ella.*

Use the Spanish term *por* when you intend the word "for" to be used for any of these meanings:

- because of, or due to
- by, through, or by means of
- during a period of time or at some time during the day
- in purpose or exchange of
- for the sake of
- as the object of an errand
- per

The following examples illustrate how the preposition *por* is used.

He went for her.	*Él fue por ella.*
I went through the whole store.	*Anduve por toda la tienda.*
I slept for two days.	*Dormí por dos días.*
I slept for two hours.	*Dormí por dos horas.*
I failed the exam for lack of sleep.	*Fallé el examen por falta de dormir.*
I bought a 2 by 4 board.	*Compré un tablero de dos por cuatro.*
We went by train.	*Fuimos por tren.*

Matching Verbs to their Subject and Tense: Infinitives and Conjugation

Though the terms may seem very technical, infinitives and conjugation are very basic to language. An *infinitive* is a word that really acts as a phrase. Infinitives in English are identified by the word "to" preceding the base form of a verb. Examples of infinitives include "to sing," "to eat," and "to write." Infinitives are what you will likely find when looking up verbs in the dictionary.

You *conjugate* a verb by changing its form to match the number of people or things (subject or pronoun) performing the verb action and the time (tense) in which the action is, was, or will be taken. These pronouns are used in the conjugation of verbs.

Singular-first (1S):

I	*yo*

Singular-second (2S)-informal:

you   *tú*

Singular-third (3S):

he   *él*
she   *ella*
you (formal)   *usted*

Plural-first (1P):

we (masculine/mixed group)   *nosotros*
we (feminine)   *nosotras*

Plural-second (2P) (Used only in Spain):

you (informal/masculine/mixed)   *vosotros*
you (feminine)   *vosotras*

Plural-third (3P):

they (masculine/mixed group)   *ellos*
they (feminine)   *ellas*
you (formal)   *ustedes*

Each infinitive has a "stem" (the basic verb) in addition to an ending. All present tense Spanish infinitives end in "ar," "er," or "ir." The verb's ending changes, however, depending on who or what is performing the action. We will use three infinitives (in present tense) to illustrate this process:

to sing   <u>*cantar*</u>
to eat   <u>*comer*</u>
to write   <u>*escribir*</u>

The Spanish word stems within these infinitives are as follows:

cant + ending
com + ending
escrib + ending

Here are the first-person singular (1S) conjugations of these verbs:

I sing   *yo canto*
I eat   *yo como*
I write   *yo escribo*

Here are the second-person singular (2S) conjugations:

you sing (informal)	*tú cantas*
you eat	*tú comes*
you write	*tú escribes*

Here are the third-person singular (3S) conjugations:

he sings	*él canta*
he eats	*él come*
he writes	*él escribe*
she sings	*ella canta*
she eats	*ella come*
she writes	*ella escribe*
you sing (formal)	*usted canta*
you eat	*usted come*
you write	*usted escribe*

These are the first-person plural (1P) conjugations of the verbs:

we sing	*nosotros(as) cantamos*
we eat	*nosotros(as) comemos*
we write	*nosotros(as) escribimos*

Here are the second-person plural (2P) conjugations:

you sing (formal)	*vosotros(as) cantáis*
you eat	*vosotros(as) coméis*
you write	*vosotros(as) escribís*

These are the third-person plural (3P) conjugations:

they sing	*ellos cantan*
they eat	*ellos comen*
they write	*ellos escriben*
they sing	*ellas cantan*
they eat	*ellas comen*
they write	*ellas escriben*
you sing (formal)	*ustedes cantan*
you eat	*ustedes comen*
you write	*ustedes escriben*

IN SEARCH OF THE INFINITIVE

After you go through the entire book once, scan through some of the chapters looking for verbs to see if you can tell what infinitive the verb came from.

The following list includes a number of Spanish infinitives. You can use this list to practice matching the verb form to the pronoun:

to buy	comprar
to study	estudiar
to speak	hablar
to take	llevar
to look at	mirar
to need	necesitar
to work	trabajar
to travel	viajar
to learn	aprender
to drink	beber
to understand	comprender
to run	correr
to read	leer
to live	vivir
to receive	recibir

note Please note that the infinitives ending in "ar" use "ar" endings (or follow the pattern of the verb *cantar*), the infinitives ending in "er" use "er" endings (following the pattern of the verb *comer*), and the "ir" verbs use "ir" endings (following the pattern of the verb *escribir*).

In conversation you may notice that the Spanish speaker drops the pronoun. The conjugation alone carries the meaning of the subject pronoun. Using the "I eat" (*Yo como*) phrase in the S1 example above, you may hear an expression that excludes the *Yo*:

I eat beans every day.   *Como frijoles todos los días.*

LISTENING FOR "SPANGLISH" TERMS

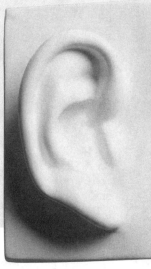

In your conversation with a Hispanic you may hear him or her say words that sound a lot like English words. Hispanics will sometimes mix English words into a Spanish sentence, or use words that are derived, not translated from English words. This language is known as *Spanglish*, a term created from the words **Spanish** and **English**. You will not have a problem when your Spanish-speaking companions use English words, but you may have a problem understanding words derived from English terms. Below are a couple of examples.

In this example, downtown is used in both the English and Spanish sentence:

I am going downtown.   *Voy al downtown.*

In this example, however, the term *brekas* is derived from the English word "brakes":

I repaired the brakes on my car.   *Reparé las brekas en mi coche.*

Summary

In this chapter we provided you with insight into some of the rules that regulate how Spanish words and sentences are to be structured, pronounced, and written. Since the intent of this book is to teach you how to pronounce Spanish words, our emphasis was on showing you what generates the Spanish sound. We described how the accent symbol plays a big role in identifying what syllables are to be stressed in the pronunciation of certain words. We also described letters and letter combinations that create unique sounds in Spanish words. We talked about the rules for assigning gender to nouns and adjectives. We ended the chapter by discussing the prepositions *para* and *por*, as well as the ways to express verbs to indicate who performed the action. Don't worry if these topics seemed a bit overwhelming. The information you've learned here, combined with the practice you'll get as you progress through this book, will help you gain control over these complexities of Spanish grammar.

In the next chapter we cover the Spanish alphabet and numbers. You learn how to pronounce the ordinal numbers, and a basic set of whole numbers, which you can use to derive whole numbers from 21 to 100,000. You also learn how to use and say numbers in areas related to money, dates, time, and units of measure.

2

Letters, Numbers, Dates, and Dollars

We learned our ABC's and how to count when we were children. We use the letters of the alphabet and numbers everyday without giving them much thought. Yet, a letter in the wrong place, or a transposed number can result in serious blunders. The alphabet and numbers play an equally important role in Spanish.

Numbers are involved in almost everything we do. We use whole and decimal numbers in conducting our financial activities, and make appointments and plot activities using whole and fractional numbers expressed as time and dates. We use ordinal numbers to talk about how our kids were first in academics in school, or how we took second place in the golf tournament. We use numbers to measure the size of things we purchase or create, and to prepare a meal according to our favorite recipe.

Where the alphabet is limited to a set amount of letters, numbers are infinite. That tends to sound a little intimidating. In mathematics you do not have to memorize the millions of results that can be derived by applying formulas to the numbers. You simply need to know the formula and how to apply it. Learning how to say Spanish numbers is much easier than that. This chapter will teach you how to easily combine a few sets of numbers to come up with the Spanish translation for almost any number you may need when speaking Spanish.

In this chapter:

- ❋ Learning the ABC's
- ❋ Learning how to count
- ❋ Using numbers to describe dates, dollars, time, and units of measure

The Alphabet

The English alphabet contains 26 letters. When we lived in Hawaii, I was surprised to discover that the Hawaiian alphabet only contains 12 letters; a, e, h, i, k, l, m, n, o, p, u, and w. The Spanish alphabet contains 26 letters, plus or minus a couple of other characters. As described in the "Letters and Letter Combinations That Create Unique Spanish Sounds" section in Chapter 1, the letter Ñ, and letter combinations CH, LL, and RR, are unofficially known as *extra alphabet*. It should be noted that the letters K and W are rarely used in the Spanish language.

You do not need to learn the Spanish alphabet to learn to speak Spanish. Yet, it is helpful to know the Spanish alphabet if someone tells you they live in *el apartamento hache* (in apartment H), for example. As you listen to the audio file that accompanies this section of the book, you will hear the pronunciation of the letter *hache* (H). The following table shows the Spanish translation for each letter of the English alphabet. The accompanying audio file pronounces the letters both in English and Spanish.

note In English each vowel has a long sound, a short sound, and each letter can have several other sounds. English vowels can be combined with other vowels to produce even more sounds. The great thing about the Spanish vowels is that, as stated in Chapter 1, they each have only one sound. If you learn the five vowel sounds you will be able to pronounce any word in Spanish.

Go to audio file 02a Alphabet.

tip Listen to the audio on the alphabet a few times, and memorize it. It can really come in handy when you least expect it.

English	Spanish	English	Spanish	English	Spanish
A	A	J	Jota	S	Ese
B	Be	K	Ka	T	Te
C	Ce	L	Ele	U	U
D	De	M	Eme	V	Ve
E	E	N	Ene	W	Doble u
F	Efe	O	O	X	Equis
G	Ge	P	Pe	Y	I griega
H	Hache	Q	Cu	Z	Zeta
I	I	R	Ere		

Numbers

Numbers come in a variety of forms, including ordinal numbers, fractions, and whole numbers. The following sections of this chapter instruct you on how to correctly express numbers through various combinations of number sets.

Ordinal Numbers

Ordinal numbers identify a position in a sequence of numbers. You use ordinal numbers, for example, to state that you live in the fourth house on the right, past the second stop sign on a given street.

Go to audio file 02b Ordinal numbers.

The following list includes the basic ordinal numbers in both English and Spanish:

first	*primero*
second	*segundo*
third	*tercero*
fourth	*cuarto*
fifth	*quinto*
sixth	*sexto*
seventh	*séptimo*
eighth	*octavo*
ninth	*noveno*
tenth	*décimo*
twentieth	*vigésimo*
hundredth	*centésimo*
thousandth	*milésimo*

Numbers have gender identification. If the written form of a number ends in O, it is masculine. If it ends in A, it is feminine. The first and third ordinal numbers, *primero* and *tercero*, are shortened when they precede a noun. If you were to be talking about your first or third auto, you would say *primer coche*, or *tercer coche*, respectively.

The eleventh and twelfth ordinal numbers are *undécimo* and *duodécimo*. Ordinal numbers thirteen through nineteen are derived by combining the Spanish translation for the "tenth" (*décimo*) and the applicable whole number between 1 and through 9. The fifteenth ordinal number, for example, is obtained by combining the Spanish terms *décimo* (tenth) and *quinto* (fifth), to form *décimoquinto*. We have included ordinal numbers twentieth, hundredth, and thousandth. Numbers from *primero* to *vigésimo* are all written as one word. From *vigésimo primero* (twenty-first) on, ordinal numbers are shown as two words. Ordinal numbers over twentieth are seldom used. Cardinal numbers are used instead.

Fractions

A fraction is created by using a whole number as the numerator and an ordinal number as the denominator. Fractions are normally expressed in numerical form, though they sometimes are spelled out, as in "I ate one-half of the sandwich." On the accompanying audio, you will hear that the Spanish translations are the same for numerical figures or spelled out fractions.

The next examples show two expressions of the same fraction. Listen to the translated sound on the number "one" in one-fourth. When "one" is used as an adjective, it is pronounced *un*. When it is used as a noun it is pronounced *uno*.

one-fourth	*un cuarto*
one-half	*la mitad*
half	*medio*
one-third	*una tercera parte*
one-eighth	*un octavo*

Whole Numbers

Although, as stated earlier, there are an infinite number of whole numbers, the following list includes only zero through twenty. The number twenty, or *veinte*, requires a unique pronunciation when combined with other numbers, as explained in the "Say it Right" tip later in this section of the chapter. Combining numbers within the "Whole Numbers" section can generate numbers from twenty to one hundred thousand.

Go to audio file 02c Whole numbers.

English	Spanish	English	Spanish	English	Spanish
zero	*cero*	*seven*	*siete*	*fourteen*	*catorce*
one	*uno*	*eight*	*ocho*	*fifteen*	*quince*
two	*dos*	*nine*	*nueve*	*sixteen*	*dieciséis*
three	*tres*	*ten*	*diez*	*seventeen*	*diecisiete*
four	*cuatro*	*eleven*	*once*	*eighteen*	*dieciocho*
five	*cinco*	*twelve*	*doce*	*nineteen*	*diecinueve*
six	*seis*	*thirteen*	*trece*	*twenty*	*veinte*

The numbers in the preceding list can be combined to create a whole range of other numbers that may be useful to you. Let's take a look at some of these combinations.

For numbers twenty-one through twenty-nine, simply add the applicable secondary number (1–9) to the prefix *veinti*. The following are a couple of examples:

twenty-three	*veintitrés*
twenty-nine	*veintinueve*

The same rule applies for incrementing numbers between thirty and ninety, except that you do not alter those numbers. You add the applicable secondary number 1–9 to the numbers between thirty and ninety with a *Y* linking the two numbers. The following includes a few examples:

thirty	*treinta*
thirty-one	*treinta y uno*
forty	*cuarenta*
forty-two	*cuarenta y dos*
fifty	*cincuenta*
fifty-three	*cincuenta y tres*
sixty	*sesenta*
sixty-four	*sesenta y cuatro*
seventy	*setenta*
eighty	*ochenta*
ninety	*noventa*

tip Listen to the pronunciation of the number "twenty." It sounds like "vein teh." Notice that when you add a unit to it and make it twenty-one, the "vein teh," spelled *"veinte,"* is pronounced like "vein tee," spelled *"veinti"* or *"veintiuno"* for twenty-one. This change only happens in the range of numbers twenty-one through twenty-nine.

Go to audio file 02d Misc numbers.

Things change when you get to the hundreds. Notice the change that takes place when we translate "one hundred" and "one hundred and five."

one hundred	*cien*
one hundred five	*ciento cinco*

Notice that "one hundred" is translated as *cien*. When you add units to the one hundred, the *cien* becomes *ciento*. Although the "hundred" remains a singular term when you state the numbers two hundred to nine hundred, the *ciento* is made plural. An exception to this is the number five hundred. It is translated as *quinientos*. Another change that takes place is in the form of *siete* and *nueve* used in seven hundred and nine hundred, respectively. They become the prefixes *sete* and *nove*, producing the translated numbers *setecientos* and *novecientos*. The following examples illustrate some of these numbers:

two hundred	*doscientos*
two hundred and five	*doscientos cinco*
three hundred	*trescientos*
three hundred fifty	*trescientos cincuenta*
four hundred	*cuatrocientos*
four hundred sixty-seven	*cuatrocientos sesenta y siete*
five hundred	*quinientos*
five hundred ninety-four	*quinientos noventa y cuatro*
six hundred	*seiscientos*
six hundred fourteen	*seiscientos catorce*
seven hundred	*setecientos*
seven hundred thirty-three	*setecientos treinta y tres*
eight hundred	*ochocientos*
eight hundred and eight	*ochocientos ocho*
nine hundred	*novecientos*
nine hundred ninety-nine	*novecientos noventa y nueve*
one thousand	*mil*
two thousand	*dos mil*
one hundred thousand	*cien mil*

The translation for the plural of "thousand" is

thousands	*miles*

In English, "million" is used when you refer to one, two, or one hundred million. The plural form is only used when one uses that term as in "I get millions of emails a day." In Spanish, "million" becomes plural in two million, three million, and so on, and *millón* loses its accent. The following are the translations for the singular and plural form of "million."

one million	*un millón*
two million	*dos millones*
millions	*millones*

note The plural expression for "thousands" is "miles." Yet, in Spanish as in English, "thousand" does not become plural when expressed in multiples of more than one. The expression for two sets of one thousand is "two thousand," not "two thousands."

Dollar Amounts

Let's apply some monetary expressions to the things we learned about numbers in the previous section. Latin American countries have their own currencies, but we will not attempt to describe transactions using those currencies. We will describe transactions using American currency.

American money transactions are normally stated in terms of "dollars" and "cents"; for example $1.98 is expressed as "One dollar and ninety eight cents." The translation and audio include the verbal expression of the dollar amounts shown here:

tip Search the Internet and compare the current value of currencies of Latin American countries to the U.S. dollar. Make sure that the website contains current information. A reliable currency conversion site is at http://finance. yahoo.com/currency/convert?amt= 1&from=USD&to=JPY&submit=Convert.

I have $3,114.63 in my checking account.	Tengo tres mil ciento catorce dólares y sesenta y tres centavos en mi cuenta de cheques.
I owe $50,300.95 on my mortgage loan.	Debo cincuenta mil trescientos dólares y noventa y cinco centavos en mi préstamo hipotecario.
I bought it for $1.98.	Lo compré por un dólar y noventa y ocho centavos.

Dates

The dates on a calendar play a very important role in our daily lives. The names of days and months will definitely come up in conversation with Hispanics, as you discuss birthdays, appointments, or scheduled activities.

Go to audio file 02e Calendar.

The days of the week are

Sunday	domingo
Monday	lunes
Tuesday	martes
Wednesday	miércoles
Thursday	jueves
Friday	viernes
Saturday	sábado

The months of the year are

January	enero	July	julio
February	febrero	August	agosto
March	marzo	September	septiembre
April	abril	October	octubre
May	mayo	November	noviembre
June	junio	December	diciembre

Dates can be expressed in several ways by combining the number that represents the calendar day, month, and year.

DATE FORMATS THROUGHOUT THE WORLD

The U.S. and some segments of the United Kingdom use the month/day/year (m/d/y), or short date format. The majority of Asian countries, as well as Portugal, South Africa (English), and Canada (French) use the y/m/d date format. Most countries with European influence and Latin American countries use the d/m/y date format. In Latin American countries, they will sometimes include the day of the week at the beginning of the d/m/y date.

What is today's date?	¿Qué es la fecha de hoy?
June 21, 2004	Veintiuno de junio, dos mil cuatro
6/21/04	seis/veintiuno/cero cuatro
The 21st day of June 2004	El día veinte y uno de junio, dos mil cuatro
What is today's day and date?	¿Qué son el día de hoy y la fecha?
Monday, June 21, 2004	lunes, veintiuno de junio, dos mil cuatro

Time

Time can be displayed under a 12-hour or a 24-hour clock. Under the 12-hour clock, you identify time by stating the hour and minutes, followed by a.m. or p.m., depending on the time of day. Fifteen-minute increments can be expressed as "quarter," "half," and "three-quarters" of an hour. Clocks at some train stations and airports will display time using the international standard notation, hh:mm:ss.

To convert time expressed in 24-hour-clock form to standard time, subtract 12 from the hours notation if the time is greater than 12. The time 23:40 would be converted to standard time as follows: 23 less 12 equals 11. The time expressed by 23:40 is therefore 11:40 p.m. The seconds are not mentioned when telling time. Some examples follow:

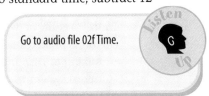

Go to audio file 02f Time.

Here are some sample discussions of time based on the 12-hour clock:

What time is it?	*¿Qué hora es?*
It is early.	*Es temprano.*
It is 1:10 a.m.	*Es la una y diez de la mañana.*

You can also express time in quarter-hour increments. Fifteen minutes is one-quarter, or *cuarto*. Thirty minutes is one-half, or *media* (it assumes the feminine gender of the hour). Forty-five minutes is three-fourths, or *tres cuartos*.

It is 11:15 p.m.	*Son las once y cuarto de la noche.*
It is 2:30 p.m.	*Son las dos y media de la tarde.*
What time does your flight arrive?	*¿A qué hora llega su vuelo?*
My flight arrives at 2:45 p.m.	*Mi vuelo llega a las dos y tres cuartos de la tarde.*
My flight arrives at 2:55 p.m.	*Mi vuelo llega a las tres menos cinco minutos de la tarde.*
I am leaving at 1:00 p.m.	*Salgo a la una de la tarde.*
I am leaving at midnight.	*Salgo a la medianoche.*
We are going to lunch at noon.	*Vamos a almorzar al mediodía.*
It is too late to eat.	*Es muy tarde para comer.*
It is early, if we call it dinner.	*Es temprano, si le llamamos cena.*

Here are some discussions of time based on the 24-hour clock:

Twenty minutes after one in the morning would be expressed as follows:

0120 hours	*cero uno veinte horas*

Six fifty p.m. would be expressed as follows:

1850 hours	*La hora dieciocho con cincuenta minutos*

Units of Measure

In this section we will introduce you to a few of the units of measure that you may come across in talking to Hispanics. We generally use the standard system in the U.S., but can see evidence

Go to audio file 02g Units of measure.

of the introduction of the metric system in product labeling. Even our cereal box tells us that it contains 25.5 ounces, or 723 grams of cereal. Most Latin American countries use the metric system of measurements.

Weight

There are not too many Spanish units of measure for weights, even when you include those terms used in science. In the following sections you will find a few sentences that include standard and metric weight terminology that may come up in a casual conversation.

Standard Weight

Most of our weight measurements involve pounds and ounces. We use these terms extensively in Chapter 7, "Shopping," where we talk about buying a pound of this and four ounces of something else. The following are a few sentences that provide the translation for standard weight terms:

There are 16 ounces in a pound.	Hay dieciséis onzas en una libra.
There are 2,000 pounds in a ton.	Hay dos mil libras en una tonelada.
Our baby weighed 8 oz at birth.	Nuestro bebé pesó ocho onzas cuando nació.
I weigh 165 pounds.	Peso ciento sesenta y cinco libras.

These sentences demonstrate how the preceding terms can be used to convey other messages related to weight:

I don't want to weigh one ounce more.	No quiero pesar una onza más.
I feel like I weigh a ton after eating that meal.	Me siento como que peso una tonelada después de comer esa comida.

Metric Weight

Most Latin American countries use the metric system of measurements. A unit of weight measurement is the kilogram, also referred to as the *kilo*. Here are some examples of sentences that include terminology related to metric units of measure:

I purchased one kilogram of corn.	*Compré un kilo de maíz.*
One kilogram equals 2.2 pounds.	*Un kilo iguala dos punto dos libras.*
A 20 ounce loaf of bread weighs 566 grams.	*Una barra de pan de veinte onzas pesa quinientos sesenta y seis gramos.*

Dimensions

Dimension is the measurement of an object in terms of its length, width, and height, or the diameter of a circle or sphere. Here are some sentences that might be used in discussions involving dimensions:

How big is the table?	*¿De qué tamaño es la mesa?*
The table is 8 feet long, 4 feet wide, and 3 1/2 feet high.	*La mesa tiene ocho pies de largo, cuatro pies de ancho, y tres pies y medio de altura.*
The table has a circular map of North and South America that is 3 feet in diameter.	*La mesa tiene un mapa circular de Norte y Sudamérica que tiene tres pies de diámetro.*

Measurements in Recipes

Recipes use the following measurements to specify how much of the ingredients are to be used in food preparation. There are two translations for teaspoon and tablespoon. The first is the translation for the utensil itself; the second translation is for the quantity the spoon is able to hold. Use a number or fraction from the "Numbers" section in this chapter to specify how much of the ingredient is to be used. The two metric measurements of volume are translated at the end of the list.

Teaspoon	*Cucharita*
Teaspoon (quantity)	*Cucharadita*
Tablespoon	*Cuchara*
Tablespoon (quantity)	*Cucharada*
Cup	*Taza*
Pint	*Pinta*
Quart	*Cuarto de galón*
Gallon	*Galón*
Liter	*Litro*
Milliliter	*Mililitro*

Here are a few examples that show how measurements are used in a recipe book:

Add 1/2 cup grated cheese.	*Añada media taza de queso rallado.*
Add 1/4 tablespoon salt.	*Añada un cuarto de cucharada de sal.*
Sprinkle one teaspoonful of cinnamon.	*Rocíe una cucharadita de canela.*

COOKING IN HISPANIC CULTURE

Hispanics prepare many succulent dishes without a recipe, or the use of kitchen utensils. The instructions have been passed on by word of mouth from generation to generation. They just mix in a *pellizco* (pinch) of this and a *puño* (handful) of that. If you are fortunate enough to be invited to participate in some feast, don't try to figure out how the food was prepared. Just go and enjoy it.

Summary

This chapter introduced you to some very important tools used in speaking Spanish. As in English, the Spanish alphabet is fixed, so it is just a matter of memorizing it. Numbers vary in form, however, depending on their use as whole numbers, fractions, or ordinal numbers. This chapter taught you how to develop any number you need by combining certain sets of number forms. The technique can be applied to generate the numbers we need to converse about topics such as dollars, time, and units of measurement. This technique will be very useful in subsequent chapters where conversational text may require the use of numbers other than those included in the text.

This also marks the end of Part I of this book. In Part II, "Talking about Your Daily Life," you learn numerous terms and techniques for speaking in Spanish about work, play, school, family, and other day-to-day aspects of your world. In Chapter 3, "Getting to Know One Another," you learn how to break down the language barrier to initiate a conversation with a Hispanic, introduce yourself, and share information about who you are and where you live.

Part II

Talking About Your Daily Life

3

Getting to Know One Another

Certain casual words and sentences can get you off to a great start in learning how to speak Spanish. Small talk allows you to break the ice with a Spanish-speaking person. The conversation does not have to be deep in order to make friends with a stranger. Say "Hola," which means "Hello" in Spanish, to the next Hispanic person you see and watch the reaction. Don't worry about the pronunciation. You will get plenty of practice later on in the book.

The words and sentences in this chapter are grouped by topics that are commonly engaged in by total strangers. There may be some redundancy in word and phrase translations within this and subsequent chapters. This is necessary because the intent is to provide you a complete set of sentences applicable to a specific circumstance.

You will find additional "small talk" words and sentences within the other chapters. Chapter 6, "Describing the Tasks of Daily Life," for example, includes sentences you can use at work to make small talk with your coworkers. Chapter 7, "Shopping," offers some casual conversation about groceries, and Chapter 9, "Managing Your Health," guides you through basic conversations you might have with friends and co-workers about your health.

The audio files present the words and sentences in the same sequence in which they're presented in this chapter. I recommend you read the English text before you play the audio file. This will help you see the arrangement of the sentences, and increase your ability to learn the Spanish related to the topic presented. After you have gone over the English text, follow these steps to make the best use of the audio files:

note If you need instruction on where to find these files go to the "Using the Audio Files" section of the Introduction.

1. Play the entire audio file and follow along in your book.

2. Pause, reverse, or fast-forward the audio file on the media player, as necessary. I recommend that the first time you hear the audio, you pause it after each phrase is pronounced in Spanish.

3. Reread the Spanish words and sentences out loud. Try to emulate the pronunciation of the Spanish words played by the media player, and note the accents and the letter "n" with a tilde above (ñ) on the written text. When you listen to the audio, you will see the role accent marks and special characters play in the pronunciation of Spanish words.

Breaking the Ice

As in any language, when you first meet someone and begin speaking with him or her, you'll probably use a series of simple, polite expressions to break the ice. The following sections describe how to say "Hello," "How are you?" and other basic introductory phrases, as well as understand the typical responses you might hear.

Before we begin, however, here are some important phrases that can bail you out of any situation in which you do not understand what the Spanish speaker says:

I do not understand.	*No entiendo.*
Please repeat what you said.	*Por favor repita lo que usted dijo.*
Or	
Please repeat what you said,	*Por favor repita lo que usted dijo,*
a little slower.	*un poco más despacio.*

FORMS OF ADDRESS

In Spanish there are two forms of address, informal and formal, when talking to a person. If you know the person really well, or if the person is the same age or younger than you, then you would use the informal or familiar address. If the person you are addressing is an elderly person, or a person that you believe warrants a high level of respect, then you would use the formal address.

The best way to learn the forms of address is by example. This chapter provides a significant number of examples on the form of address. Subsequent chapters will use whatever form of address is appropriate without further explanation.

Basic Greetings and Their Follow-up

Use any of the following words or sentences as a basic greeting depending on the time of day. "Hello" can, of course, be used at any time of day and in any situation. Each group of questions includes possible Spanish responses.

Hello	*Hola*
Good morning	*Buenos días*
Good afternoon	*Buenas tardes*
Good evening	*Buenas noches*
Good night	*Buenas noches*

A good follow-up to the basic greeting is to ask, "How are you?" This expression can be used at any time, regardless of the gender of the person you are speaking to. In English you often get an identical response to a "How are you?" greeting; in other words, if you say, "How are you?" the person you've spoken to may respond, "How are you?" In Spanish, people more commonly respond to the greeting with a phrase that states how they are, such as "I am fine."

The Spanish phrase "How are you?" translates into a variety of sentences depending on the gender, age, or level of respect warranted by the person you are addressing.

Go to audio file 03a Greetings.

tip The words in *italics* are in the audio file.

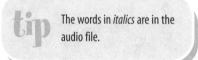

Remember what you learned in Chapter 1 about feminine and masculine nouns:

Masculine	Nouns end in the letter *O*
Feminine	Nouns end in the letter *A*

The formal and informal translations for the word *you* are

Informal address	*tú*
Formal address	*usted*

Below you will find the words "you all" included as part of the greeting. Although it is recognized that not everybody that speaks English uses "you all" in lieu of the word "you," it is used here to demonstrate how the singular Spanish words for "you"—"tú" and "usted"—become the single term "ustedes" when you use the plural form of "you."

THE ORIGIN OF USTED

At some point you may see the letters Ud. and Uds. on some document or book. These are abbreviations for, and are pronounced as, *usted* and *ustedes*. Usted originated from *vuestra merced*, which literally means "Your Mercy," or "Your Highness." *Vuestra merced* was used in addressing royalty. *Usted* and *ustedes* are sometimes abbreviated Vd. and Vds. which is a shortened version of *vuestra merced*.

Informal Greetings

If you are addressing one person, you ask:

How are you?   ¿Cómo estás?

Or you can ask:

How are you doing?   ¿Cómo te va?

If you are addressing more than one person:

How are you all?   ¿Cómo están?
Or
How are you all?   ¿Cómo les va?

Formal Greetings

You can use the informal form of address when speaking to anyone that you know well and would be comfortable calling by their first name. Use the formal form of address if you feel that you should address the person as "Sir" or "Madam." When in doubt, or if you do not know the person well enough, use the formal form of address.

If you are addressing one person:

How are you?   ¿Cómo está usted?

If you are addressing more than one person:

How are you all?   ¿Cómo están ustedes?

If the person is a male who warrants a high level of respect, you would ask:

How are you, sir?   ¿Cómo está usted, señor?

If the person is a female who warrants a high level of respect, you would ask:

How are you, ma'am?   ¿Cómo está usted, señora?

If the female is single, or if you don't know the marital status, you would ask:

How are you ma'am?   ¿Cómo está usted, señorita?

Responses to Your Greeting

Some replies to the "How are you?" greeting are as follows:

Very well.	Muy bien.
Very well, thank you.	Muy bien, gracias.
Okay or fine.	Bien.
So-so.	Así así.
Bad.	Mal.
Very bad.	Muy mal.

Sometimes the response may be in the form of a question. In this version of that reply, the speaker uses informal address to reply to one person:

Very well, and you?   ¿Muy bien, y tú?

If the response is to more than one person:

Very well, and you all?   ¿Muy bien, y ustedes?

Using formal address, here is the response to one person:

Very well, and you?   ¿Muy bien, y usted?

If the response is to more than one person:

Very well, and you all?   ¿Muy bien, y ustedes?

TECHNIQUES FOR MEMORIZING AND RECALLING TERMS

Follow any or all of these techniques to improve your ability to memorize Spanish terms and phrases:

* Select words and phrases that describe things that interest you. Listen to them on a media player a few times.

* Repeat the English and Spanish words and phrases until you are able to pronounce the Spanish words and phrases correctly.

* Write down the English and Spanish words and phrases that you want to learn. Practice writing them in Spanish from memory.

* Try to pronounce Spanish terms without hearing the audio file, then check out your pronunciation by playing the audio files.

* Use the things around you as your flash cards. To do that, memorize the Spanish names of objects that interest you and try to recall their names as you see them. Say the names of trees, houses, the sky, mountains, and other objects as you are driving around in your car.

* Memorize phrases that describe situations you encounter on your way to work, to the market, or around the house.

* If you see a person walking down the street as you are driving, say to yourself such things as "Hello, my name is..." or "What is your name?" in Spanish.

* Expand your practice base to other phrases.

* Practice your Spanish on someone who understands it.

Talking About Who You Are

If you get a response to your greeting and you want to initiate a conversation, introduce yourself using some of the following sentences. They will probably lead to an exchange of other information.

Exchanging Names

A good start is to just state your name without trying to translate it:

My name is...   *Mi nombre es...*

If you are addressing one person using informal address, you can ask:

What's your name?	*¿Cómo te llamas?*

Using formal address, you ask:

What's your name?	*¿Cómo se llama?*

If you are addressing more than one person, the question is:

What are your names?	*¿Qué son sus nombres?*

The person, or persons, you greet will usually just state their name(s). The response is the same for an informal or formal question:

My name is María	*Me llamo María.*
Our names are José and María.	*Nuestros nombres son José y María.*
Our names are José and María.	*Nos llamamos José y María.*

Describing Where You Are From

If you want to tell the person(s) you are talking to where you are from, and you are in the city where you reside, you say:

I live in this city.	*Vivo en esta ciudad.*

Suppose you live in Jacksonville, Florida, for example. You would say:

I live in Jacksonville, Florida.	*Yo vivo en Jacksonville, Florida.*

If you are in another country and you want to say that you are from a certain state in, or from the United States, you can say:

I live in the state of Florida.	*Yo vivo en el estado de Florida.*
I live in the United States of America.	*Yo vivo en los Estados Unidos.*

If you are addressing one person, and you are interested in knowing where the person is from, you would ask the following based on the form of address. Using informal address, the question would be this:

Where are you from?	*¿De dónde eres?*

Here is the question, using the formal form of address:

Where are you from?   *¿De dónde es usted?*

If you are addressing more than one person, the question would be:

Where are you all from?   *¿De dónde son ustedes?*

Summary

In this chapter, you learned how to make that initial contact with a Hispanic person. You learned details about when to use the formal and informal forms of address. If you learn this material, you will be able to talk about who you and your Hispanic friend are and where you are from.

Now that you and your Hispanic friend know a little bit about each other, you may want to get more specific about your respective families. The next chapter provides you extensive translated material on talking about the family and other relationships. You will be able to discuss marital status, what the family members do for a living, how the kids are doing in school, and how to say, "I love you" to that special somebody.

Audio Files

Discussing Your Family and Friends

In this chapter:

* Talking about love and marriage
* Discussing family, their jobs, and school
* Describing total family interrelationships
* Talking about friends
* Expressing terms that touch the heart

Hispanics are very family oriented. They form strong ties with immediate as well as with extended family members. In many homes several generations of the same family live together. In most traditional Hispanic families, the father, as the head of the family, is responsible for providing for the family, and the mother is responsible for the home. Children generally live at home longer than in other cultures. Hispanics tend to marry and have children at a younger age. When one family member hurts, the whole family feels it. Parents instill in their children a moral responsibility to help other members of the family who might be experiencing health or financial problems. They teach their children to respect their elders. They stress that they should never forget their heritage and their language regardless of the levels of success they may achieve.

Hispanics like to celebrate. When there is a reason to celebrate, the whole family celebrates. They celebrate special occasions with music, food, drink, and dance. Grandparents, uncles, aunts, cousins, and other relatives gather from all over to participate in celebrations of birthdays, graduations, and weddings. Religious events such as baptisms and first communions are very important in the Hispanic community. They celebrate major holidays, such as Easter, Christmas, New Year's Day, and their Independence Day with colorful festivals, known as fiestas.

This chapter provides a number of sentences that will get you off to a good start in a social conversation in Spanish about your marital status, children, and other family members. You will be able to talk about the kind of work that members of your family are engaged in, and how your relatives are doing in school. The subject of family will definitely trigger questions and comments from your Hispanic counterpart. You learn phrases and sentences you'll use to discuss your extended family, friends, and acquaintances. The chapter ends on a "mushy" note (to use a familiar American English expression), by providing you with a short selection of affectionate terms that can either make a lot points for you or get you in trouble, depending on how (and with whom) you use them.

EL ALMUERZO OR NOON MEAL

One of the ways that Hispanics reinforce their strong family ties is through the noon meal, known as *el almuerzo*. It is the main meal in Hispanic homes. Household family members are expected to participate in this meal. They will usually take a two-hour break from their job or school to take part in el almuerzo. During this time the family talks about how things are going at work, school, or within the family. They discuss any problem a family member may be having. It is not uncommon to invite close friends to partake of the noon meal and to participate in social conversation over a cup of coffee after the meal.

Discussing Marital Status

A discussion about family will more than likely be preceded by talk about marital status, spouses, or significant others. So let's begin this chapter with some social conversation examples that you can use to inquire about and respond to questions about marriage. Then, we'll learn some expressions used to describe other types of serious relationships.

Go to audio file 04a Love and marriage.

The following is a series of questions and responses on marital status. You can use these to inquire about someone else's marital status. The questions can also be posed to you. There are two different translations for the single question, "Are you married? (*Estás casado, estás casada*)" depending on the gender of the addressee.

Male addressee:

Are you married?	*¿Estás casado?*

Female addressee:

Are you married?	*¿Estás casada?*

Possible responses may be:

Male:

I am married.	*Estoy casado.*
I am married to (insert name)	*Estoy casado con* (insert name)

Female:

I am married.	*Estoy casada.*
I am married to (insert name)	*Estoy casada con* (insert name)

Male:

I am not married.	*No estoy casado.*

Female:

I am not married.	*No estoy casada.*

Male:

I am single.	*Estoy soltero.*

Female:

I am single.	*Estoy soltera.*

Male:

I am separated.	*Estoy separado.*

Female:

I am separated.	*Estoy separada.*

Male:

I am divorced.   Estoy divorciado.

Female:

I am divorced.   Estoy divorciada.

The following sentences might be used in a discussion about a wedding or anniversary:

I understand you got married.	Entiendo que te casaste.
Congratulations!	¡Felicidades!
Congratulations on your marriage.	Felicidades en tu matrimonio.
When did you get married?	¿Cuándo te casaste?
I got married on June 15.	Me casé el quince de junio.
Did you have a large wedding?	¿Tuviste una boda grande?
I had ten attendants.	Tuve diez asistentes.
Did you have a wedding reception?	¿Tuviste un banquete de bodas?
Where did you go on your honeymoon?	¿Adónde fuiste en tu luna de miel?
We went to Acapulco.	Fuimos a Acapulco.
How long have you been married?	¿Cuánto tiempo has estado casada?
I have been married eight years.	He estado casada por ocho años.
We celebrated our eighth wedding anniversary.	Celebramos nuestro octavo aniversario de boda.

Here are some terms used to describe the wedding and members of a typical wedding ceremony:

Wedding	La boda
Groom	El novio
Bride	La novia
Wedding ceremony	La ceremonia matrimonial
Attendants	Los asistentes
Maid of honor	La dama de honor
Best man	El padrino de boda
Bridesmaids	Las madrinas de boda
Groomsmen	Los padrinos de boda

note The distinction between "best man" and "groomsmen" is that the best man is the singular *padrino*, referred to as *el padrino de boda*, or the best man.

Flower girl	*La florera*
Ring bearer	*El portador del anillo*
Wedding dress	*El traje de novia*
Wedding party	*El cortejo nupcial*
Wedding cake	*El pastel de boda*
Wedding march	*La marcha nupcial*

A HISPANIC WEDDING

The religious and civil ceremonies in Hispanic and typical U.S. weddings are similar. The proceedings are performed within the context of the religious or legal process, rather than cultural traditions. There may be some difference in the musical instruments used and the music that is played during the wedding ceremony. Music at Hispanic weddings is loud and generally includes trumpets, guitars, drums, and a large bass guitar known as *el guitarrón*. Both cultures have an after-wedding celebration where friends and family gather to eat, drink, and dance, or just listen to the music. There are significant differences in the food served and music played at the after-wedding reception. This difference exists even among the different countries that are part of the Hispanic community. One of the things that distinguishes a Mexican wedding from a U.S. wedding is the wedding march, or *la marcha*. This is not the "Here comes the bride" march played preceding the wedding ceremony. *La marcha* is a follow-the-leader dance led by a man and a woman chosen by the bride. Men and women line up in separate lines and each holds the shoulders of the person in front of him/her. They march to music played by *Mariachis* or a DJ. The two lines weave in and out of each other, split up, rejoin, and somehow manage to match up with the respective partner at the end of the march. If you get the opportunity, join in. All you have to do is not lose the person in front of you.

Other Long-term or Significant Relationships

Let's begin this segment with sentences used to discuss the kind of friendship that brings people together, in love, which sometimes leads to marriage.

Go to audio file 04b Love and marriage.

Do you have a girlfriend?	*¿Tienes tú una novia?*
Do you have a boyfriend?	*¿Tienes tú un novio?*
Yes, I do.	*Sí, tengo.*
No, I do not.	*No, no tengo.*

We have been going with each other for 3 years.	*Hemos estado saliendo el uno con el otro por tres años.*
We plan to get engaged in the spring.	*Tenemos intención de comprometernos en matrimonio en la primavera.*
We want to be friends for life.	*Queremos ser amigos por vida.*

Talking About Your Spouse and Children

If you or the person you are talking to are married, the conversation may turn to a discussion of your spouses and children. In this section you will find sentences that will allow you to talk about what the members of your respective households do for a living, and how the children are doing in school. In "Describing Other Relationships," later in this chapter, you learn expressions used for talking about other members of your immediate and extended family.

Go to audio file 04c
Household family.

This section includes the Spanish terms used to name family members.

I have a wife.	*Tengo una esposa.*
I have a husband.	*Tengo un esposo.*
Do you (plural) have children?	*¿Tienen niños?*

If you are asking a single parent, the question and answer would be as shown in the next two entries:

Do you have children?	*¿Tienes niños?*
I do not have children.	*No tengo niños.*
We have no children.	*No tenemos niños.*

note There are many different translations for the words child, children, kids, sons, and daughters. The more commonly used Spanish term for all of the above is *niño* (male), *niña* (female), and *niños* (plural male and female).

We have children.	*Tenemos niños.*
We have one child.	*Tenemos una niña.*
I have a child.	*Tengo un niño.*
We have a son.	*Tenemos un hijo.*
Our son's name is…	*Nuestro hijo se llama…*
Our son looks like my husband.	*Nuestro hijo se parece a mi esposo.*

Our son is 10 years old.	Nuestro hijo tiene diez años de edad.
Our son is tall for his age.	Nuestro hijo es alto para su edad.
We have a daughter.	Tenemos una hija.
Our daughter's name is…	Nuestra hija se llama…
Our daughter looks like her mother.	Nuestra hija se parece a su mamá.
Our daughter is 15 years old.	Nuestra hija tiene quince años de edad.
Our daughter is beautiful.	Nuestra hija es bella.
We have a son and a daughter.	Tenemos un hijo y una hija.
My wife is expecting a baby.	Mi esposa está esperando a un bebé.
We have twins.	Tenemos gemelos.
We have triplets.	Tenemos trillizos.
My wife suffered a miscarriage.	Mi esposa sufrió un malparto.
My mother-in-law lives with us.	Mi suegra vive con nosotros.
My father-in-law lives with us.	Mi suegro vive con nosotros.
Our family consists of me, my husband, and our dog.	Nuestra familia consiste de mí, mi esposo, y nuestro perro.
We love our children.	Amamos a nuestros niños.
Our children tell us that they love us.	Nuestros niños nos dicen que nos aman.
Our children are well-behaved.	Nuestros niños son bien comportados.
Our children do not always behave.	Nuestros niños no siempre se portan bien.

The following series of questions can be used to inquire about brothers, sisters, and the composition of the family within their household. Only a couple of examples are shown for the number of siblings involved. Translation for numbers can be found in Chapter 2, "Letters, Numbers, Dates, and Dollars." The plural for brother and sister is, as in English, identified by the letter "s" at the end of the word.

Go to audio file 04d
Household family.

We wish that love would always reign in every family relationship, and that it would last forever. Unfortunately, that is not always the case. Separation and divorce are facts of life. You may encounter such situations in your social conversation with adults or perhaps even with children, who seem to be the most affected by marriage malfunctions.

Do you have a mommy and a daddy at home?	*¿Tienes tú una mamá y un papá en casa?*
Yes, my mommy and daddy live at home.	*Sí, mi mamá y papá viven en casa.*
No, my parents are divorced.	*No, mis padres están divorciados.*
No, my parents are separated.	*No, mis padres están separados.*
I live with my mother.	*Vivo con mi madre.*
I live with my father.	*Vivo con mi padre.*
My mother is a single parent.	*Mi madre está sin pareja.*
My father is a single parent.	*Mi padre está sin pareja.*
I live with an older sister.	*Vivo con una hermana mayor.*
Do you have any brothers and sisters?	*¿Tienes tú hermanos y hermanas?*
No, I do not have any brothers or sisters.	*No, no tengo hermanos ni hermanas.*
Yes, I have one brother and two sisters.	*Sí, tengo un hermano y dos hermanas.*
How many brothers and sisters do you have?	*¿Cuántos hermanos y hermanas tienes tú?*
I have:	*Tengo:*
one brother.	*un hermano.*
one sister.	*una hermana.*
one brother and one sister.	*un hermano y una hermana.*
one brother and two sisters.	*un hermano y dos hermanas.*

If you are addressing a child who is in the company of one or more children, the following will apply:

Is that your little brother?	*¿Es él tu hermanito?*
Is that your little sister?	*¿Es ella tu hermanita?*
Yes, he is my brother.	*Sí, él es mi hermano.*
Yes, she is my sister.	*Sí, ella es mi hermana.*

Talking about Your Family Members' Occupations

The working habits in family life have changed. The head of household is no longer the only one that works. Other family members are working by choice or because of necessity. Teenagers will get a job after school in order to buy the latest sound or video equipment. Wives are no longer confined to the role of raising the children. Day care has made it possible for both parents to go out and work. In some cases, the husband stays at home to clean house and raise the children. Here you will find sentences that will allow you to discuss these different scenarios.

This section's discussion of occupations is limited to simply stating that the household family members are employed at something. It does not provide details about the type of employment they are involved in. In Chapter 6, "Discussing Work and Other Activities of Daily Life," you will find an extensive list of occupations.

Go to audio file 04e Family occupations.

The following text can be used by either a husband or a wife. The first two examples apply to the husband and wife, respectively:

I am the sole breadwinner in our house.	Soy el sostén económico exclusivo en nuestra casa.
I am the only one that works at our house.	Soy la única que trabaja en nuestra casa.
Where do you work?	¿Dónde trabaja usted?
I am self-employed.	Trabajo por cuenta propia.
I work for the State.	Trabajo para el Estado.
We work in an office.	Trabajamos en una oficina.
Where do your children work?	¿Dónde trabajan sus niños?
Our teenage children work at a fast food restaurant.	Nuestros niños adolescentes trabajan en un restaurante de comida rápida.
My daughter works in a movie theater after school.	Mi hija trabaja en un cine después de escuela.
My son is a lifeguard at the city pool.	Mi hijo es un salvavidas en la piscina de la ciudad.
Our teenage children do not work.	Nuestros niños adolescentes no trabajan.

The following examples alternate between sentences spoken by the husband and wife:

My wife also works.	Mi esposa también trabaja.
My husband has a part-time job.	Mi esposo tiene un trabajo de medio tiempo.
My wife works, and I take care of the children.	Mi esposa trabaja, y yo cuido a los niños.
My husband has a temporary job.	Mi esposo tiene un trabajo temporal.

Describing School Grade Levels

In discussions about the family, invariably, the conversation turns to how children are doing in school. We want to know what grade they are in, and how they are doing. If they are college age, we want to know whether they are attending college and what they are majoring in.

Go to audio file 04f Family and school.

The following examples provide you with sentences useful in talking with other parents about their children.

Do you have any children in school?	*¿Tienes niños en la escuela?*
My 7 and 9 year-old children are in school.	*Mis niños de siete y nueve años están en la escuela.*
Our daughter is in junior high school.	*Nuestra hija está en la Escuela Intermedia.*
My brother is a junior in college.	*Mi hermano es un estudiante de penúltimo año en la universidad.*
My sister is a senior in high school.	*Mi hermana es una estudiante de último año en la escuela secundaria.*
Our 16 year-old son is in high school.	*Nuestro hijo de dieciséis años está en la escuela secundaria.*
Our 19 year-old twins are attending the university.	*Nuestros gemelos de diecinueve años asisten a la universidad.*
Are the kids doing well in school?	*¿Están los niños haciendo bien en la escuela?*
They are doing quite well, thanks.	*Están haciendo bastante bien, gracias.*
My son is struggling with math.	*Mi hijo lucha con la matemática.*

HISPANIC SCHOOL TERMS

The Spanish word for "college" can refer to any school from kindergarten through grade 12. The term does not just apply to a university or college. The following is the translation of this word:

college   colegio

If your Hispanic companion tells you that one of her family members is going to college, you may want to ask what grade level that person is in.

You may have the opportunity to talk to Hispanics about their school attendance, interests, and goals. Here you will find material you can use to initiate such a dialogue.

Are you in school?	*¿Estás tú en la escuela?*
Yes, I go to a primary school.	*Sí, voy a una escuela primaria.*
I attend a technical school.	*Asisto a una escuela técnica.*
I go to a vocational school.	*Voy a una escuela vocacional.*

If the person is not in school, the response to the question "Are you in school?" would be:

No, I am not in school.	*No, no estoy en la escuela.*

or:

I am taking a break from school.	*Tomo un descanso de la escuela.*
I am a freshman in high school.	*Soy un estudiante del primer año en la escuela secundaria.*
I am a sophomore in college.	*Soy un estudiante del segundo año en la universidad.*
I am a junior in junior college.	*Soy un júnior en la escuela semisuperior.*
I am a senior at the university.	*Soy un estudiante del último año en la universidad.*
I graduated from high school.	*Me gradué de la escuela secundaria.*
I graduated from college.	*Me gradué de la universidad.*

Discussing University Majors

A discussion about school beyond high school may lead to a discussion of what the student is studying or majoring in. You can also use the following responses to state what you are majoring in, if you are still in school:

Go to audio file 04g School majors.

What are you studying?	*¿Qué estás estudiando?*
I have not chosen a major, yet.	*No he escogido una asignatura principal, todavía.*
I don't know what I want to be.	*No sé lo que quiero ser.*
I am majoring in journalism.	*Me especializo en el periodismo.*

Here is a partial list of university majors:

Accounting	la Contabilidad
Agricultural Economics	la Economía Agrícola
Art	el Arte
Biology	la Biología
Biochemistry	la Bioquímica
Business Management	la Dirección Empresarial
Chemistry	la Química
Computer Science	la Informática
Economics	la Economía
Education	la Educación
Engineering—Chemical	la Ingeniería—Químico
Engineering—Civil	la Ingeniería—Civil
Engineering—Electrical	la Ingeniería—Eléctrico
Engineering—Mechanical	la Ingeniería—Mecánico
English	el Inglés
Finance	las Finanzas
Information Systems	los Sistemas De Información
International Business	el Comercio Internacional
Marketing	la Mercadotecnia
Mathematics	las Matemáticas
Medicine	la Medicina
Music	la Música
Nursing	la profesión de Enfermera
Pharmacy	la Farmacia
Physical Education	la Educación Física
Psychology	la Psicología
Sociology	la Sociología
Spanish	el Español

Describing Other Relationships

In this section you learn terms, phrases, and sentences used to describe and discuss extended family and other relationships that exist beyond the immediate family.

These relationships include grandparents, uncles, aunts, cousins, and stepchildren, as well as relationships that go beyond family, such as the strong bond of friendship.

BARRIO HOSPITALITY

In the Hispanic *barrio* where I grew up, it seemed that most households had large families. I don't know how they were able to fit all those kids in such small houses. What was incredible to me was the fact that when relatives or friends from out of town visited, they were never sent to a restaurant to eat a meal or to a motel to spend the night. My neighbors somehow found a way to feed and accommodate their guests in their small houses. Hispanics will sacrifice everything they have to take care of you. The saying that "they will give you the shirt off their back" is true.

Extended Family Relationships

In this section we will describe relationships that exist between a Hispanic and kin, or blood relationships, outside the Hispanic's household. This includes grandparents, uncles, aunts, and cousins.

Go to audio file 04h Extended family.

We all have wonderful memories of our grandparents, and like to refer to how nice it is, or was, to have them around. They never got on our case when we failed, and were always there when we hurt. Some of you may be grandparents, and know how wonderful it is to have a grandchild come up and tell you that they love you. Let's talk a little bit about the best people on earth.

Tell me about your grandfather.	*Cuéntame sobre tu abuelo.*
Tell me about your grandmother.	*Cuéntame sobre tu abuela.*
My grandpa, or grandma:	*Mi abuelito, o mi abuelita:*
is very nice to me.	*es muy amable conmigo.*
gives me hugs.	*me da abrazos.*
loves me.	*me ama.*
gives me money.	*me da dinero.*
gives me presents.	*me da regalos.*

tells me stories.	me dice cuentos.
makes good food.	hace buena comida.
makes me feel well when I am ill.	me hace sentir bien cuando estoy enfermo.
My grandparents gave me a car when I was in school.	Mis abuelos me dieron un coche cuando estaba en la escuela.
My grandfather excelled in business.	Mi abuelo sobresalió en el negocio.
My grandfather taught me a good work ethic.	Mi abuelo me enseñó buena ética de trabajo.
My grandmother sang opera professionally.	Mi abuela cantó ópera profesionalmente.
My grandmother helped me get started in my business.	Mi abuela me ayudó a empezar mi negocio.

If you happen to talk to someone who is a grandparent or great-grandparent, get comfortable. They will want to talk about how great their grandchildren or great-grandchildren are. Be prepared to require some further translations, because your Hispanic companion will pour out more words than we can possibly include in this book!

I have three grandsons.	Tengo tres nietos.
I have a granddaughter.	Tengo una nieta.
My grandchildren are the smartest kids in the world.	Mis nietos son los niños más sabios en el mundo.
My granddaughter is the prettiest girl in town.	Mi nieta es la chica más bonita en la ciudad.
Our grandson is the most handsome child around.	Nuestro nieto es el niño más bien parecido dondequiera.
I have a great-grandson.	Tengo un bisnieto.
I have four great-granddaughters.	Tengo cuatro bisnietas.
My great-grandkids are twice as smart and good-looking as my grandkids.	Mis bisnietos son el doble de sabios y guapos que mis nietos.

You also may find yourself engaged in a discussion of other family members. Here are some sample sentences you might use:

I have one uncle and two aunts.	Tengo un tío y dos tías.
My uncle is my mother's brother.	Mi tío es el hermano de mi madre.
My aunts are my father's sisters.	Mis tías son las hermanas de mi papá.

My uncle and two aunts have four children.	*Mi tío y dos tías tienen cuatro niños.*
I have two female cousins.	*Tengo dos primas.*
I have two male cousins.	*Tengo dos primos.*

Other Family Relationships

In this segment we are going to expand the extended family to include "step" relationships created by someone marrying a person with children from another relationship. We will include a couple of sentences on relationships created through foster care and adoption.

Go to audio file 04i Other family and friends.

I adopted my wife's son by a former marriage.	*Adopté al hijo de mi esposa por un anterior matrimonio.*
I adopted my husband's daughter by a former marriage.	*Adopté a la hija de mi esposo por un anterior matrimonio.*
I have a stepfather.	*Tengo un padrastro.*
I have three stepchildren.	*Tengo tres hijastros.*
I have one stepson and two stepdaughters.	*Tengo un hijastro y dos hijastras.*
This is my stepdaughter.	*Ésta es mi hijastra.*
I have a stepbrother.	*Tengo un hermanastro.*
I have two stepsisters.	*Tengo dos hermanastras.*
I have an adopted son.	*Tengo un hijo adoptado.*
I take care of a foster child.	*Cuido a un niño adoptivo.*
I am an adopted son.	*Soy un hijo adoptado.*
I am a foster child.	*Soy un niño adoptivo.*

Friends and Acquaintances

The word friend has a special meaning to Hispanics. There is a strong bond between friends, as long as there is trust between them. If a Hispanic calls you *amigo*, consider yourself fortunate. It means that the Hispanic believes that you are trustworthy and is willing to give you the shirt off his back. Friendship is an attribute that bonds Hispanics to each other and to those that treat them with respect and dignity.

I like to play golf with my friends.	*Me gusta jugar al golf con mis amigos.*
My friend and I go shopping.	*Mi amiga y yo vamos de compras.*
My friend works at the bank.	*Mi amiga trabaja en el banco.*

I received an email from a friend in Costa Rica.	Recibí un correo electrónico de un amigo en Costa Rica.
I can trust my friend to watch our house when we go on vacation.	Puedo confiar en mi amigo para cuidar de nuestra casa cuando vamos de vacaciones.
Our friend calls us up to make sure we are okay.	Nuestro amigo nos llama para confirmar que estamos bien.
My best friend will do anything for me.	Mi mejor amigo hará cualquier cosa para mí.
We became friends when we shared a room at the hospital.	Nos hicimos amigos cuando compartimos un cuarto en el hospital.
My friend and I are going out to lunch.	Mi amigo y yo vamos a almorzar.
Who is your best friend?	¿Quién es tu mejor amiga?
You are my best friend.	Tú eres mi mejor amiga.
A friend does anything for a friend.	Un amigo hace cualquier cosa para un amigo.
We are not real friends; we barely know each other.	No somos realmente amigos; apenas nos conocemos.
They are just acquaintances.	Son simplemente conocidos.

Terms of Endearment

What do you say to someone whom you really care about? It all depends on the level of affection you wish to convey. There are varying degrees of love that one can express. Here are some terms and expressions related to this sensitive subject.

I love you.	Te amo.
I love you with all my heart.	Te quiero de todo corazón.
I adore you.	Te adoro.
I like you.	Me gustas.
I care for you.	Te quiero.

Many of the terms shown in the following list can be used to get someone's attention, in lieu of using the person's name. If the Spanish term has a different literal meaning, it is shown in parentheses. These terms can also be used to express to someone that he or she holds a special place in

Go to audio file 04j Terms of endearment.

note Some Spanish terms of endearment can have several translations, as in the *Te adoro* example you see translated here. In the examples presented in the audio that accompanies this section of the chapter, the English word is repeated in the audio in order to indicate a variation of the respective term. The gender is alternated as much as possible. Words ending in "a" refer to female; words ending in "o" refer to male.

your heart, by using "You are my," or simply saying "My" as shown in the following examples.

You are my:	*Tú eres mi:*
My:	*Mi:*
Sweetheart	Amorcito (little love)
My sweetheart	Mi corazoncito (little heart)

Even though *amorcito* and *corazoncito* end in the letter "o," those terms can also be applied to the female gender.

Sweetheart or darling	*Querida* (one that I like)
Sweetheart	*Corazón* (heart)
My life	*Mi vida*
My lover	*Mi amante*
Beloved (In the plural form)	*Bien amados*
Beloved (adj)	*Amado* (loved one)
My prince	*Mi príncipe*
My princess	*Mi princesa*
My little princess	*Mi princesita*
My queen	*Mi reina*
My king	*Mi rey*

Hispanic married people often call each other names that may not seem very endearing to a bystander, but nevertheless they are used as expressions of affection and love.

Husbands refer to their wife as:

Old lady	*Vieja (old—female gender)*
My old lady	*Mi viejita (my little old one)*
My chubby one	*Mi gordita* (this comes from *gorda*, which means fat)

In Mexico, the following expressions are used to refer to one's wife, based on her complexion:

My little dark one	*Mi prietita*
My fair-skinned one	*Mi güerita*

Wives refer to their husband as:

Old man	Viejo
My chubby one	Mi gordito
Dark one (Used in Mexico)	Prieto

DEVELOPING YOUR OWN TRANSLATION LISTS

As you read this book and listen to the audio, jot down the words and phrases related to a topic that you may be interested in speaking about in Spanish. Write down the English and Spanish words side by side. If you want to talk about your house, for example, use words and phrases from Chapter 5, "Talking About Your Home and Personal Belongings." As you go through the various chapters, develop new translation lists and add words and phrases that apply to previously developed lists.

The following example is a brief translation list of terms you can use to introduce yourself to someone, and talk about your spouse and your children. This example shows how you can use material from two chapters and several audio files to create a single list. It identifies the audio files that contain the words and phrases for easy reference. Fill in the Spanish translation in the area to the right of each English word or phrase.

TALKING ABOUT CHILDREN WITH SOMEONE YOU JUST MET

Write out and say the Spanish words or phrases here

Audio file 03a

Hello   _____

How are you?   _____

My name is (name)   _____

Audio file 04a

I am married.   _____

I am married to (insert name)   _____

How long have you been married?	_____
I have been married for (enter number of) years.	_____
Audio file 04c	
Do you have children?	_____
My wife is expecting a baby.	_____
We have a daughter.	_____
Audio file 04f	
Our daughter is in junior high school.	_____

Summary

In this chapter you learned Spanish terms, phrases, and sentences you can use to talk about marriage, spouses, different family members, and levels of family relationships. You were exposed to language Hispanics might use to describe what their families do for a living, and how their children are doing in school. This chapter also talked about the strong bond that exists between Hispanic families and how this bond extends to close friends. When you see a man lean over and whisper something to his wife, and if she giggles, you know that he probably told her, "*Mi gordita, Te adoro* (My little chubby one, I love you)."

In this and previous chapters of this book, I have referred to people living in small houses in the *barrio* where I grew up. That is no longer the case. Many Hispanics live in large, nice homes. The next chapter provides extensive translated material that you can use to describe your home and inquire about your friend's home.

Audio Files

Talking About Your Town, Home, and Personal Belongings

It is natural to want to know about someone else's living environment, activities, and interests. Social conversations can readily turn to discussions about what city or town we live in, what kind of house we have, and what is inside and outside our house. This chapter will provide you with words you can use to describe the city or town where you reside, the details on the size of your house, and how many rooms your house has. It will allow you to describe what each room is used for, and what is in each room. This chapter will provide you an extensive list of personal items and what they are used for. Finally, it provides you very useful and practical translated text that you can use in hiring a Hispanic, or to rent out a house or apartment you might have.

5

In this chapter:

* Talking about the town where you live
* Describing your home
* Talking about clothes, TV, and pets
* Hiring domestic help
* Renting out an apartment or house

Talking about Your Town, City, or Neighborhood

The following sentences only relate to the physical features of your municipality. They do not address the government organization structure of the municipality. Translated terms and sentences for the political side of the local municipality will be presented in Chapter 13, "The Political World."

In Chapter 4, you read about the term *barrio*, one of the Spanish words for neighborhood. Unfortunately, in movies and television programming, this term has sometimes been associated with a poor, crime-ridden neighborhood. Consequently, many of us who were raised on "the wrong side of the tracks" like to think that we left the *barrio*. Not so! As long as we live in a neighborhood, we live in a *barrio*.

> **tip** Keep in mind that learning the translations will not only help you speak Spanish, it will also help you understand what someone is saying in Spanish.

> **Say It Right**
> Have fun trying to roll the R's in *barrio*. This will help you pronounce any word with double R's in it. If you need more practice on rolling your R's, go to the "Letters and Letter Combinations That Create Unique Spanish Sounds" section in Chapter 1, "The Rules— Short and Sweet."

Describing Where You Live

Here are some sentences you might use to tell others where you live and ask about their home place:

> **Listen Up**
> Go to audio file 05a The town.

I live in a small town.	Vivo en un pueblo pequeño.
I live in a city.	Vivo en una ciudad.
I live in a large city.	Vivo en una ciudad grande.
Do you live in a small town?	¿Vives tú en un pueblo pequeño?
Do you live in a city?	¿Vives tú en una ciudad?

The response to these two questions can be "yes," "no," or one of the first three preceding sentences.

I live in a small town without skyscrapers.	Vivo en un pueblo pequeño sin rascacielos.
I live in a large city with skyscrapers.	Vivo en una ciudad grande con rascacielos.
I live on a ranch.	Vivo en un rancho.

Talking about the Neighborhood

Everyone's neighborhood is unique. Here are some sentences that might be used in a casual conversation to describe a neighborhood:

I live in a quiet neighborhood.   *Vivo en un barrio tranquilo.*

In the following translations is the basic phrase "I live on a street" accompanied by a number of phrases you could use to describe the street (the audio will play a completed sentence):

I live on a street:	*Vivo en una calle:*
that is congested.	*congestionada.*
with good lighting.	*con buena iluminación.*
where there is plenty of construction.	*donde abunda la construcción.*
that is very quiet.	*muy tranquila.*
with wide sidewalks.	*con aceras anchas.*
with a traffic light on the corner.	*con un semáforo en la esquina.*

Here are phrases you can use with "I live":

I live:	*Vivo:*
on a dead-end street.	*en una calle sin salida.*
on a one-way street.	*en una calle de una vía.*
by a highway.	*por una carretera.*
by a freeway.	*por una autopista.*

Describing Your Home

This section provides you the words you can use to initiate a conversation with a Hispanic person about what type of house you both live in. It will allow you to describe the type of structure you live in, including whether it's single level or multi-level, and its size. It provides a lead-in for a subsequent detailed discussion on the rooms in the house.

TALKING ABOUT THE HOUSE

In my travels through several large cities in Mexico and Panama City in Central America I discovered that many Hispanics own very large, luxurious houses. The majority of the Hispanic population in those areas, however, lives in poverty. Many of them live in shacks made out of cardboard. Most of those that migrate into the U.S. are from the second group. These people fully understand what a great luxury a house truly is.

If you show a genuine interest in them, you will discover that Hispanics are proud people who are very thankful for what they have. They will not have a problem talking about what little they have or hope to have someday. The material in this chapter takes these factors into consideration, and enables you to ease into a discussion of the house you live in without offending anybody.

In this section we are also going to talk about the components of a typical home. You'll learn sentences that will help you talk about the different rooms in your house and the furnishings and appliances you use each day. You'll also learn expressions and sentences that will be useful when talking about your yard and garage.

Go to audio file 05b
The house.

Talking About the House

Tell me about the house that you live in.   *Cuénteme sobre la casa en la que usted vive.*

If you ask the previous question, you may get one of the following possible responses. You can also use the responses to describe the type of house you live in.

Possible responses:

I live in a one-story house.	*Vivo en una casa de un piso.*
I live in a two-story house.	*Vivo en una casa de dos pisos.*
I live in a condominium.	*Vivo en un condominio.*
I live in a high rise condominium.	*Vivo en un condominio de gran altura.*
I live in an adobe house.	*Vivo en una casa de adobe.*
My house is big.	*Mi casa es grande.*
My house is small.	*Mi casa es pequeña.*
I live in a new house.	*Vivo en una casa nueva.*

I live in an old house.   Vivo en una casa vieja.

My house is very cozy.   Mi casa es muy acogedora.

Describing the Details of Your Home

The minimum requirement for a building to be
called a home is that it provide a place to eat
and a place to sleep. Homes come in different
sizes and include a variety of rooms.

You can use the sentences you learn here to
describe the various rooms in your home and the
furniture that is in them. We've even included
some furniture lists, so you can talk about the
furnishings within your home, too.

Speaking of the Main Rooms

In this section, you learn some sentences you
might use when taking about the different rooms
within your home, their size, and the furnishings
they contain. We begin with the living room:

We use the living room   Usamos la sala para
to entertain guests.   entretener a
                                los invitados.

Another name for living room is *sala de estar*.

We use our living room   Usamos nuestra sala
as a family room.   como un cuarto
                                familiar.

Our family watches   Nuestra familia ve
television in the living   televisión en la sala.
room.

Here are two sentences that describe the physical
description of the living room:

The living room is large.   La sala es grande.

My living room is very   Mi sala es muy
small.   pequeña.

Speaking of...

In this section you get to
apply the instruction on determining gender provided in the
"Effect of Gender on Nouns" section of
Chapter 1. Inanimate objects such as the
rooms in the house and household items
described in the following section are con-
ferred either a masculine or feminine gender when preceded by the articles "the," "a,"
or "an." You do not have to worry about
when to apply the masculine or feminine
gender. The explanations provided are just
for your information. The translated sentences show the proper gender.

note   You can substitute the
name of any piece of fur-
niture you desire for those
shown in the lists. Just go to any English-to-
Spanish dictionary, or a translation on the
Internet, and select the Spanish term for the
piece of furniture you want.

Go to audio file 05c Living
room.

Listen Up

LIVING ROOM FURNISHINGS

In the following phrase, you can replace the listed furniture with other furniture from a Spanish dictionary, if you want.

My living room has:	Mi sala tiene:
a sofa (or a couch)	un sofá
an upholstered chair	una silla tapizada
an ottoman	un otomán
a reclining armchair	un sillón recostable
a coffee table	una mesita para servir café
a cocktail table	una mesita para servir cóctel
a lamp	una lámpara
a fireplace	una chimenea
an entertainment center	un centro de entretenimiento
a television	una televisión
a CD player	un reproductor de discos compactos
a DVD player	un lector de DVD

The master bedroom is a luxury not found in the majority of Hispanic homes in Latin American countries. Only the wealthier Hispanics will have a master bedroom in their homes. But here are some sentences and phrases you can use to discuss any of the bedrooms in your home.

SPANISH TERMS FOR "BEDROOM"

There are four Spanish words commonly used for bedroom. They are *recámara* (literal translation, bedchamber), *dormitorio* (dormitory), *alcoba* (alcove), and *cuarto de dormir* (sleeping quarters). The two most commonly used terms in Latin American countries are *recámara* and *cuarto de dormir*. You will get a chance to learn how to pronounce these words by listening to and practicing with the audio file that accompanies this section.

These sentences can be used to describe the bedrooms and their furnishings:

My house has a big master bedroom.	*Mi casa tiene una recámara principal grande.*
My house has two bedrooms.	*Mi casa tiene dos cuartos de dormir.*
My bedroom has:	*Mi recámara tiene:*
a balcony.	*un balcón.*
a king-size bed.	*Una cama de tamaño extra.*
a queen-size bed.	*una cama de tamaño de reina.*
a double bed.	*una cama de matrimonio.*
a twin bed.	*una cama gemela.*
a closet.	*un ropero.*
a dresser.	*un tocador.*
two night stands.	*dos mesas de noche.*
an armoire.	*un armario.*
The bedrooms have carpet on the floor.	*Los dormitorios tienen alfombra en el piso.*

Go to audio file 05d Bedrooms.

THE MATRIMONY BED

A double bed is also called a *cama de matrimonio*, which literally means "matrimony bed."

As a practical matter, most families eat most of their meals in a "non-formal" setting where there is just a table and chairs. However, here are some sentences you might use to discuss a more formal dining area:

Go to audio file 05e Dining and study.

My house has a spacious dining room.	*Mi casa tiene un comedor espacioso.*

My dining room has:	Mi comedor tiene:
a china cabinet.	una vitrina de la porcelana china.
a table.	una mesa.
six chairs.	seis sillas.
a chandelier.	un candelabro.
candle holders.	unos candeleros.

A HOME OFFICE OR STUDY

Many homes today have a home office or study; here are some terms you might use to discuss this room in your house:

My house has a study.	Mi casa tiene un cuarto de estudio.
My study has:	Mi cuarto de estudio tiene:
a desk.	un escritorio.
a chair.	una silla.
a computer.	una computadora.
a bookshelf.	un estante de libros.
books.	unos libros.

Discussing the Kitchen, Bath, and Utility Rooms

The modern American kitchen is probably the room in a house that has the most electrical gadgets. The homes of many Hispanics in other countries aren't loaded with these luxuries. In fact, some have only a wood-burning stove and a sink, and possibly no running water. Newly arrived Hispanics may be very curious about the modern contraptions they see in your kitchen. Here are some useful sentences for talking about the kitchen:

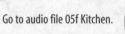

Go to audio file 05f Kitchen.

My house has a tiny kitchen.	Mi casa tiene una cocina chiquita.
My kitchen has linoleum on the floor.	Mi cocina tiene linóleo en el piso.
My kitchen has tile on the floor.	Mi cocina tiene baldosa en el piso.

SPANISH NAMES FOR TILE

There are three different translations for tile depending on where it is set. If the tile is "floor tile," it is called *baldosa*. Tile used on walls is called *azulejo*. Roof tile, as you'll see later in the "Hiring Maintenance and Repair Workers" section toward the end of this chapter, translates to *teja*. You will learn the various pronunciations when you get to the sections that contain the use of these terms.

My kitchen has:	Mi cocina tiene:
a stove.	una estufa.
a wood-burning stove.	una estufa que quema leña.
an electric range.	una estufa eléctrica.
a gas range.	una estufa que quema gas.
a refrigerator.	un refrigerador.
a freezer.	un congelador.
a refrigerator and freezer combination.	una combinación de refrigerador y congelador.
cabinets.	unos gabinetes.
a sink.	un fregadero.
a dishwasher.	un lavaplatos.
a microwave.	un microondas.
a self-cleaning oven.	un horno autolimpiador.
a table.	una mesa.
chairs.	unas sillas.

EL BAÑO

The literal translation for the noun *baño* is bath, bathroom, or shower. Just as in English, many Hispanics use this term to identify a restroom, even if that "bathroom" contains only a toilet and a sink.

Here are some sentences you might use to discuss the fixtures found in a typical bathroom:

My house has a bathroom in the master bedroom.	Mi casa tiene un cuarto de baño en el dormitorio principal.

Go to audio file 05g Bath and utility rooms.

My bathroom has:	Mi cuarto de baño tiene:
a bathtub.	una bañera.
a shower.	una regadera.
a jacuzzi.	un jacuzzi.
a toilet.	un inodoro.
wall tile.	el azulejo.

Jacuzzi is a relatively new word in the Spanish language. The audio file in this section correctly pronounces jacuzzi with the H sound for the letter J, or "ha coosy." You may hear this term pronounced with a Y, or "ya coosy" on Spanish programs. The pronunciation in the audio file is the correct pronunciation.

The laundry room can be any room that is used to wash and dry clothes. It may be in the garage, or a utility room. The following are sentences and phrases that describe the appliances and other things that are normally found in a laundry room.

My house has a laundry room.	Mi casa tiene un cuarto del lavadero.
My laundry room has:	Mi cuarto del lavadero tiene:
a washer.	una máquina de lavar.
a dryer.	una secadora.
a tub.	una tina.
an iron.	una plancha eléctrica.
an ironing board.	una tabla de planchar.

The Yard

Your home's environment begins right outside your door. Many of us like to speak with friends and co-workers about our yard and landscaping. The following sentences might be spoken in a casual combination about your yard:

Go to audio file 05h Yard.

My house has a yard.	Mi casa tiene una yarda.

My yard has:	Mi yarda tiene:
a lawn.	un césped.
volcanic rock.	la roca volcánica.
a fence.	una cerca.
a brick wall.	una pared de ladrillo.
a rock wall.	una pared de piedra.
a sprinkler system.	un sistema de regadío.
trees.	unos árboles.
shrubs.	unos arbustos.
flower beds.	unos macizos de flores.
a pond.	un estanque.
a swimming pool.	una piscina.

The Garage

Most garages house more than just automobiles. In fact, sometimes our cars are parked in what little space is left after we fill our garage with all the other stuff. You can use the following sentences to describe the contents of your garage.

Go to audio file 05i Garage.

IS IT A "GARAGE" OR A "SHOP"?

In English the term "garage" refers to a part of a private house where a car is stored, as well as to a commercial garage where cars are repaired. In Spanish there are different terms for each type of garage; *garaje* refers to your home's garage, and *taller mecánico* means "mechanic's shop."

My house has a one-car garage.	*Mi casa tiene un garaje de un coche.*
My house has a two-car garage.	*Mi casa tiene un garaje de dos carros.*
I keep my automobile in my garage.	*Mantengo mi automóvil en mi garaje.*
I store yard equipment in my garage.	*Guardo equipo de yarda en mi garaje.*
My garage is full of junk.	*Mi garaje está lleno de trastos viejos.*
I need to clean out my garage.	*Necesito limpiar mi garaje.*
How much will you charge me to clean my garage?	*¿Cuánto me cobras para limpiar mi garaje?*
I take my auto to the garage for repairs.	*Llevo mi auto al taller mecánico para las reparaciones.*

These sentences demonstrate what some of the different types of vehicles are called in Spanish:

We own a 4-door sedan.	*Tenemos un sedán de cuatro puertas.*
I drive a convertible sports coupe.	*Manejo un cupé deportivo convertible.*
Our family has a sport utility vehicle.	*Nuestra familia tiene un vehículo utilitario deportivo.*
I have an antique car.	*Tengo un coche antiguo.*
We have a truck.	*Tenemos un camión.*

Talking about Personal Possessions

In this section you learn sentences that will be helpful for discussing other common elements of your daily life. These include phrases and item names that fall into three categories—clothes, the television, and pets. There are hundreds, maybe thousands of personal items that we could include in this section, but that isn't necessary in order to teach you the basics of talking about your possessions. Once you learn how to use the introductory phrases you learn here, you can apply the Spanish term for any item to those phrases.

Describing Clothes

This section of the chapter includes a sampling of phrases that can be used with a list of articles of clothing. Each phrase is constructed so you can just add the clothing item name at the end of the phrase. At the end of the list of items you will find several interrogative phrases and a reference to the associated audio examples that demonstrate how to change the inflection on the noun to make it sound like a question.

Go to audio file 05j Clothes.

Using Singular Nouns

Use these phrases when applying singular nouns, such as "dress," "jacket," and so on in sentences discussing items of clothing:

I need to buy:	Necesito comprar:
I want to buy:	Quiero comprar:
I bought:	Compré:
I have:	Yo tengo:
I want to give you:	Quiero darle:

Here are some terms used to describe single items of clothing:

a dress.	un vestido.
a skirt.	una falda.
a blouse.	una blusa.
a jacket.	una chaqueta.
underwear.	la ropa interior.
a sweater.	un suéter.
a coat.	un abrigo.
a shirt.	una camisa.
a dress shirt.	una camisa de etiqueta.
a tie.	una corbata.
a belt.	un cinturón.
a pair of pants.	unos pantalones.
a pair of socks.	un par de calcetines.
a pair of stockings.	unas medias.
a pair of shorts.	unos pantalones cortos.

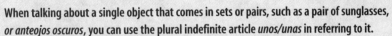

THE IMPLIED PAIR

When talking about a single object that comes in sets or pairs, such as a pair of sunglasses, or *anteojos oscuros*, you can use the plural indefinite article *unos/unas* in referring to it.

I bought a new pair of sunglasses.   *Compré unos anteojos oscuros nuevos.*

You use the singular indefinite article *un/una* if you include *par*, the Spanish word for "pair" in the sentence.

I bought a new pair of sunglasses.   *Compré un par de anteojos oscuros nuevos.*

Using Plural Nouns

To make nouns plural in Spanish, both the articles *el/la* and *un/una* have to change. They change to *los/las*, and *unos/unas*. The noun itself changes as well, as described in this section.

Add "s" to words that end in a vowel:

> "blouse," or *la blusa*, becomes *las blusas*

Add "es" to words that end in a consonant.

> "a watch," or *un reloj*, becomes *unos relojes*

In words that end in "z", change the "z" to "c" and add "es":

> "the pencil," or *el lápiz*, becomes *los lápices*

In nouns that end in "s", change the article to plural:

> "the umbrella," or *el paraguas*, becomes *los paraguas*

For nouns that end in "ión" with an accent, change the article to plural, drop the accent, and add "es":

> "airplane," or *el avión*, becomes *los aviones*

Add "es" and an accent to nouns that end in an unstressed syllable:

> "volume," or *el volumen* becomes *los volúmenes*

Notice that in the following sentence, the word *ropa* does not have an S at the end of it. The reason is that *ropa*, the Spanish word for "clothing," is already plural.

> *I want to give you children's clothing.*   *Quiero darle ropa de niños.*

In the "question" form, each translated noun should be pronounced with the interrogative inflection. Listen to the "interrogative sound" in the following examples.

Do you have a skirt?	*¿Tiene usted una falda?*
Do you own a tie?	*¿Posee usted una corbata?*

Talking About Television

The television is in a realm of technology that is rapidly changing. It is often difficult to keep up with the evolving terminology in English. No translation has been developed for many of the new features and capabilities that come with the new television sets. You will often hear Hispanics say the English name for some of these features.

Go to audio file 05k The television.

The following sentences can be used to talk about what kind of television set you have.

We have a black and white television set.	*Tenemos una televisión blanquinegro.*
Do you have a TV?	*¿Tiene usted una televisión?*
I have a color television set.	*Tengo un set de televisión en colores.*
I have a 19-inch television set	*Tengo una televisión de diecinueve pulgadas.*

A television in Spanish is generally referred to as a *tele,* or *televisión.* These sentences (and the accompanying audio file) demonstrate the use of each of these terms:

I watch a lot of television.	*Miro muchísima televisión.*
I do not watch much television.	*No miro mucha televisión.*
I enjoy watching the news on TV.	*Me gusta mirar las noticias en la tele.*
I enjoy watching the soap operas on TV.	*Me gusta mirar las telenovelas en la tele.*
I enjoy watching sports on TV.	*Me gusta mirar deportes en la tele.*
I control how much television my children watch.	*Controlo cuánta televisión miran mis niños.*
Do you control what your children watch on TV?	*¿Controla usted lo que sus niños miran en la tele?*

Discussing Pets

Many people love to talk about their pets. In this section of the chapter, you learn to use a variety of statements related to those animals that are commonly held as domestic pets. Translation of other animal names can be found in Chapter 11, "Discussing Science and Computers," in the "Simple Conversation About Science" section under "Miscellaneous— Animals."

Go to audio file 051 Pets.

I have:	*Tengo:*
a dog.	*un perro.*
two cats.	*dos gatos.*
a canary.	*un canario.*
several canaries.	*varios canarios.*
a parakeet.	*un periquito.*
a fish.	*un pez.*
a horse.	*un caballo.*
a rabbit.	*un conejo.*
a bird.	*un pájaro.*

a gerbil.	un gerbo.
a turtle.	una tortuga.
a hamster.	un hámster.
a guinea pig.	un cobayo.
I take my pets to the veterinarian to be vaccinated.	Llevo a mis mascotas al veterinario para ser vacunadas.
It is important that pets be vaccinated for rabies.	Es importante que las mascotas sean vacunadas para la rabia.
My children love to play with our pets.	A mis niños les gusta jugar con nuestras mascotas.
My bird makes me happy when he sings.	Mi pajarito me hace feliz cuando canta.
My poodle follows me like a shadow.	Mi caniche me sigue como una sombra.
My German shepherd is the best watchdog.	Mi perro pastor alemán es el mejor guardián.
I am in love with my Saint Bernard's eyes.	Estoy enamorada con los ojos de mi perro de San Bernardo.

Hiring Maintenance and Repair Workers

As the Hispanic population spreads all over the world, you will find that there are many Hispanic people looking for employment. Old misperceptions about Hispanics being limited in skills to menial labor and farm work are quickly disappearing. Many Hispanics are skilled in construction, and the performance of maintenance and repair work. They are involved in the construction of homes all over the Western and Southwestern part of the United States. When we are able to communicate with Hispanics in their own language, we are able to understand the wide range of skills, talents, and work experiences they possess.

MUSIC AND WORK

Hispanics are generally a happy people. If necessity forces them to have to work hard in an extreme environment, they would rather sing than worry about how badly life treats them. It is not uncommon to see Hispanics working in the hot sun at some construction site or out in the field with their radios blaring out some "Ranchera," or Mexican folk song. Next time you drive by one of those sites, roll down your windows and just listen to the music.

This section includes a description of repairs, or maintenance work your house or property may need. It provides sentences that can be used to hire someone, and to provide instruction on the repairs or maintenance required.

Go to audio file 05m Hiring repairmen.

Describing Maintenance Problems and Necessary Repairs

The first stage of hiring a skilled maintenance worker might involve discussing what repairs and maintenance your home and property need. Here are some sentences used in these discussions:

My house needs:	Mi casa necesita:
a few minor repairs.	algunas reparaciones menores.
major repairs.	reparaciones mayores.
some yard work.	trabajo de yarda.
roof repairs.	reparaciones del techo.
roof tile repairs.	reparaciones de la teja del techo.
a new roof.	un techo nuevo.
paintwork.	una pintura.
painting of the outside trim.	una pintura del adorno exterior.

Asking about Specific Skills

Here are some sentences used to ask about specific skills used in the performance of maintenance and repair:

Can you:	¿Puedes tú:
repair the plumbing problems?	reparar los problemas de plomería?
repair the electrical problems?	reparar los problemas eléctricos?
repair the heating problems?	reparar los problemas calefactorios?
repair the air conditioning problems?	reparar los problemas del aire acondicionado?
repair the problems with the sewage system?	reparar los problemas con el sistema de alcantarillado?
paint the trim on my house?	pintar el adorno en mi casa?
paint my house?	pintar mi casa?
work on my yard?	trabajar en mi yarda?
prune my trees and shrubs?	podar mis árboles y mis arbustos?
mow my lawn?	cortar mi césped?
repair the roof on my house?	reparar el techo en mi casa?
replace the roof on my house?	reponer el techo en mi casa?

Renting Out an Apartment/House

If you have an apartment or house that you want to rent, the sentences you learn here will help you convey information about the rental property.

Go to audio file 05n Renting out apt.

I have an apartment for rent.	*Tengo un apartamento de renta.*
I have a one-bedroom apartment for rent.	*Tengo un apartamento de una recámara de alquiler.*
I have a two-bedroom apartment for rent.	*Tengo un apartamento de dos recámaras de renta.*
I have a house for lease.	*Tengo una casa para arrendar.*
The lease cost is $800 per month.	*El costo de arriendo es ochocientos dólares por mes.*
The rent is due on the first day of the month.	*La renta vence el primer día del mes.*
There is a late payment charge, if rent is not paid by due date.	*Hay un cargo de pago retrasado, si la renta no se paga para la fecha de vencimiento.*

The late payment charge is $50. — *El cargo de pago retrasado es cincuenta dólares.*

The apartment is furnished. — *El apartamento está amueblado.*

The apartment is unfurnished. — *El apartamento está sin muebles.*

The apartment will be available in two months. — *El apartamento estará disponible en dos meses.*

If a date, number, or amount is involved in a statement, refer to Chapter 2, "Letters, Numbers, Dates, and Dollars," for translation of dates and numbers.

note In this section we will introduce you to terms related to the word "rent," a noun. This word translates to *alquiler* in Latin American countries other than Mexico. The phrase "to rent," or "rent out" translates to *alquilar*. In Mexico the noun "rent" is usually called *renta*, and "to rent" translates to *rentar*. The word "lease" is translated *arriendo*, and "to lease" is *arrendar*. The leasing process is translated as *arrendamiento*. This latter term is used throughout Latin America to identify a rental action where a lease is executed.

In order to rent this apartament you must sign a lease.	Para alquilar este apartamento tú debes firmar un contrato de arrendamiento.
The term of the lease is one year.	El término del arrendamiento es un año.
A deposit of $300 is required.	Un depósito de trescientos dólares es requerido.
The rent payment does not include the cost of utilities.	El pago de renta no incluye el costo de servicios públicos.
The rent payment includes the following utilities:	El pago de renta incluye los siguientes servicios públicos:
water.	el agua.
gas.	el gas.
electricity.	la electricidad.
garbage collection.	la colección de basura.

Summary

This chapter provided you an array of translations that can be very useful in social conversation about almost every aspect of where you live. It included Spanish terms, phrases, and sentences you can use to describe the town that you live in, your house and all its rooms, and the majority of furniture and appliances that are found in each room. You learned how to discuss such topics as clothes, watching television, and pets. This chapter also provided you language you can use to hire a Hispanic to make repairs or do other work on your house and to negotiate the leasing or renting out of an apartment or house.

You will draw upon the material you learned in this chapter as you work through the next chapter, "Describing the Tasks of Daily Life." Invariably, social conversation in the workplace turns to discussions on the home, and that new piece of furniture we just bought, or what needs to be repaired. In the next chapter you will learn how to engage in social conversation about your job, where you work, who you work with and for, and what goes on in the workplace. You will also learn to talk about the best part of the workday—when you get off of work. You will be able to discuss what you are going to do after work, whether it is some chore or some form of recreation.

Audio Files

- ❏ 06a The work-place
- ❏ 06b Your job
- ❏ 06c Your workplace
- ❏ 06d Management
- ❏ 06e Office supplies
- ❏ 06f The employees' work experience
- ❏ 06g Recreation—active sports
- ❏ 06h Recreation—spectator sports
- ❏ 06i After-work activities

Discussing Work and Other Activities of Daily Life

In this chapter, you learn how to talk about many aspects of daily life, including your job, workplace, and co-workers. We all know that when we are treated as part of the team we can perform better. This chapter helps you learn to talk about the workplace, job safety, office supplies, and all aspects of the job with Hispanic co-workers. You also learn how to discuss after-work interests and activities, including sports, running errands, making a quick trip to the mall, attending some function, or making plans for the weekend.

With the terms, phrases, and sentences you learn in this chapter, you will be able to converse with Hispanics, not only about their prior job experience, performance, and current responsibilities, but also of their after-work interests. When there is friendly interaction between the boss and employees, and among employees, the morale will improve and productivity will increase.

6

In this chapter:

* Talking about your job, workplace, and work environment

* Asking employees and co-workers about past work experiences

* Conversing about recreational sports activities

* Discussing after-work activities

Talking About Work

Everybody, including CEOs and top executives, engage in some conversations about the place they work, the work they do, their co-workers, offices, and other aspects of working life. New employees explain about past work experiences and describe their families. Management and co-workers help orient new employees to the job by explaining safety rules and the process for ordering office supplies. And job satisfaction and working conditions are important topics, both between co-workers and between management and non-management personnel. In this section of the chapter, you learn many of the terms, phrases, and sentences used to discuss these and other aspects of working life.

THE IMPORTANCE OF WORKPLACE CONVERSATIONS

It would benefit management to get into some social conversation with subordinate employees about their job, the workplace, and their thoughts on management and office policy. At a minimum, management should inquire about an employee's family, or ask if there is anything they can do for the employee. It gives the employees a feeling of "belonging," and makes them feel that management actually cares. It is also good for employees to know who their peers are. Non–English-speaking Hispanics are often left out of this interaction because of their inability to speak English. The translations you learn in this chapter help you overcome barriers that may have prevented you from participating in these important conversations with Hispanic managers, employees, and co-workers.

Describing Where You Work

The workplace can be an office, a factory, a construction site, or a farm field. This section of the chapter presents conversational text about several different kinds of businesses that may constitute "the workplace."

Go to audio file 06a The workplace.

In this company we do mostly office work.	En ésta compañía hacemos principalmente trabajo de oficina.
In this shop we do maintenance work.	En éste taller hacemos trabajo de mantenimiento.
This company is in the construction business.	Ésta compañía está en el negocio de la construcción.
We are landscape architects.	Somos arquitectos que diseñamos jardines.
Our factory manufactures toys.	Nuestra fábrica produce juguetes.
Our store sells furniture.	Nuestra tienda vende muebles.
We are a government office.	Somos una oficina del gobierno.
How long have you worked for our company?	¿Cuánto tiempo hace que usted trabaja para nuestra compañía?
I have worked here for ten years.	He trabajado aquí por diez años.

Describing Job Satisfaction

The job is probably the subject that is most discussed, next to family. Everyone has to work. We all have a job we love, hate, or can tolerate. Someone who enjoys working is generally more willing to talk to others about all the challenging assignments they get and how well they do them.

Go to audio file 06b Your job.

Likewise, someone who really enjoys his or her job is more inclined to want to know about what others do for a living.

This section provides material that can be used to discuss various aspects of the job.

Do you like your job?	¿Te gusta tu trabajo?
I love my job.	Me encanta mi trabajo.
I like the hours.	Me gustan las horas.
I enjoy the work I do.	Me da placer con el trabajo que hago.
What do you like best about your job?	¿Qué te gusta más de tu trabajo?
I work independently.	Trabajo independientemente.
My boss makes me feel that I am important.	Mi patrón me hace sentir que soy importante.
I feel that I am making a contribution to the company.	Siento que contribuyo para la compañía.
How are you doing on the job?	¿Cómo te va en el trabajo?
Is there anything you need?	¿Hay algo que tú necesitas?
What can I do for you?	¿Qué puedo hacer para ti?

The response may be one of the following:

I am doing fine.	*Todo está bien.*
I have difficulties doing my job.	*Tengo dificultades haciendo mi trabajo.*
I need more training.	*Necesito más entrenamiento.*
Be patient with me.	*Ten paciencia conmigo.*
Give me the opportunity to learn the job.	*Dame la oportunidad para aprender el trabajo.*

As a manager, you might ask a Hispanic employee about his or her job satisfaction like this:

Do you like working here?	*¿Te gusta trabajar aquí?*

Possible responses:

Yes, I like working here.	*Sí, me gusta trabajar aquí.*
No, I do not like working here.	*No, no me gusta trabajar aquí.*
I am looking for another job.	*Busco otro trabajo.*

If you are a manager and you want to pursue the issue of why the employee does not like working for your company, the following may help:

Why do you dislike working here?	*¿Por qué no te gusta trabajar aquí?*

The employee could have multiple reasons for dissatisfaction with his or her place of employment. Here are some possible responses:

The pay is too low.	*El sueldo es demasiado bajo.*
I have not been trained on my job.	*No he sido entrenado en mi trabajo.*
I do not understand the English instructions I get.	*No entiendo las instrucciones que se me dan en inglés.*
I feel that no one cares about me.	*Siento que a nadie le importa de mí.*

Describing Workplace Conditions

You also may have the need to speak with a Hispanic co-worker, employee, or manager about the working conditions in your area. Here are some sentences you might use to report problems or benefits associated with the condition of your workplace:

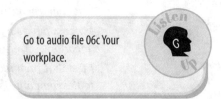

Go to audio file 06c Your workplace.

Is the workplace okay?	¿Está bien el lugar de trabajo?
Is the office okay?	¿Está bien la oficina?
Is the shop okay?	¿Está bien el taller?
Is there any problem?	¿Hay algún problema?
It is cold.	Está frío(a).

If the reference is to the feminine term *oficina*, the response would be *Está fría*, as indicated by the (a).

It is hot.	Está caliente.
It needs ventilation.	Necesita ventilación.
It is congested.	Está congestionado(a).
It is noisy.	Hay mucho ruido.
It is unsafe.	Hay mucho peligro.
Do you need any equipment?	¿Necesitas algún equipo?
Do you need any tools?	¿Necesitas herramientas?
Do you have any complaints?	¿Tienes algunas quejas?
I need a new computer.	Necesito una computadora nueva.
Some equipment is not working.	Algún equipo no funciona.
I'm missing tools.	Me faltan herramientas.
I need new tools.	Necesito herramientas nuevas.
My chair is broken.	Mi silla está quebrada.
The coffeepot doesn't work.	La cafetera no opera.

As an employer, you might respond to complaints with these sentences:

I will look into it.	Lo investigaré.
I will get back with you.	Volveré con usted.
I will fix the problem.	Arreglaré el problema.
Come into my office.	Entra en mi oficina.
Let us talk some more.	Hablemos algo más.
We will look for a solution.	Buscaremos una solución.

Greeting a New Employee

We all know that first impressions are critical. It is important that a company make a new employee feel that he or she is a valued addition to the company staff. A personal greeting by the big boss makes a big impression on new employees. The new employee should be provided information on office policies and procedures, as well as information on what assistance is available should he or she need any job related help. This section provides you a few sentences that you can use to greet the new employee, and to inform him or her of some of the office policies and procedures.

Go to audio file 06d Management.

Here are some words you can use to introduce yourself to a newly hired Hispanic employee.

Hello, welcome to our company.   *Hola, bienvenido a nuestra compañía.*

If you are a supervisor, when you introduce yourself to a subordinate Hispanic employee, it is proper to state your form of address, such as Mr., Mrs., or Ms. in English, followed by your name. If you want to use the Spanish form of address, here are the translations:

Mr.	*señor*
Mrs.	*señora*
Miss	*señorita*
Ms.	*señora*
My name is Mr. Brown.	*Mi nombre es señor Brown.*
I am your supervisor.	*Soy su supervisor.*

Here are some other expressions you might use when first meeting a new Hispanic employee and introducing him or her to your company and its policies:

Do you speak English?	*¿Habla inglés?*
Do you understand English?	*¿Entiende usted el inglés?*
Can you read English?	*¿Puede leer usted inglés?*
The orientation packet includes the following in Spanish:	*El paquete de orientación incluye lo siguiente en español:*
company policy.	*la política de compañía.*
office procedures.	*los procedimientos de la oficina.*
safety rules.	*las reglas de seguridad.*
We will provide you classroom training.	*Te proveeremos entrenamiento de la clase.*
We will give you on-the-job training.	*Te daremos entrenamiento en el trabajo.*
A tutor will help you.	*Un tutor te dará ayuda.*
We will evaluate you annually.	*Te evaluaremos anualmente.*

See me if you:.	*Veme si tú:*
need anything	*necesitas cualquier cosa.*
have any problem.	*tienes cualquier problema.*
believe someone treated you unfairly.	*crees que alguien te trató injustamente.*

Requesting Office Supplies

The office supply inventory will vary depending on the nature of the business and the equipment the office includes. This section provides translation for some of the basic supplies found in a typical office environment.

Go to audio file 06e Office supplies.

We use:	*Usamos:*
We need to buy:	*Necesitamos comprar:*
Please go buy:	*Por favor ve a comprar:*
Please do not waste:	*Por favor no malgastes:*
paper.	*el papel.*
manila folders.	*las carpetas manila.*
pencils.	*los lápices.*
scotch tape.	*la cinta adhesiva Scotch.*
staplers.	*las engrapadoras.*
staples.	*las grapas.*
a staple remover.	*un removedor de la grapa.*
an inkjet cartridge.	*un cartucho de inyección de tinta.*
laser cartridges.	*los cartuchos del láser.*
a bulletin board.	*un tablero de anuncios.*
note pads.	*los blocs para apuntes.*
envelopes.	*los sobres.*
paper clips.	*los sujetapapeles*
a calendar.	*un calendario.*
a dictionary.	*un diccionario.*
a thesaurus.	*un tesauro.*

Discussing Previous Work Experiences

You may discover that some of your Hispanic employees or peers have extensive work experience in areas that might be helpful to your company. Here you will find phrases and sentences that you can use to initiate a discussion about their work experience in the country they came from.

What kind of work did you do in your country?	*¿Qué clase de trabajo hizo usted en su país?*
I owned my own business.	*Fui dueño de mi negocio.*
I owned a grocery store.	*Fui dueño de una tienda de comestibles.*
I owned a construction business.	*Fui dueño de un negocio de la construcción.*
I owned a franchise business that sold tacos.	*Fui dueño de un negocio de franquicia que vendía tacos.*
I worked as a farmhand.	*Trabajé como un trabajador agrícola.*
I worked on a ranch.	*Trabajé en un rancho.*
I worked in an office.	*Trabajé en una oficina.*
I worked in a factory.	*Trabajé en una fábrica.*
I worked in a store.	*Trabajé en una tienda.*
I was a professional.	*Fui un profesional.*

You may want to pursue the "professional" job by asking:

What is your educational background?	*¿Cuál es su fondo educativo?*

A possible response will be:

I have a degree in accounting.	*Tengo un título en la contabilidad.*

note There are many highly educated Hispanics working in farm fields, factories, or as custodians. They immigrate to this country in search of a better future for their children, and work at menial jobs simply because they cannot speak English. They are intelligent and could learn to do higher-level work with little training, depending on what they studied. You may want to explore this source of talent. The material in this section will help you do that.

Go to audio file 06f The employees' work experience.

The "School Grade Levels" section of Chapter 4, "Discussing Your Family and Friends," includes a partial list of translated university majors.

| *What kind of work did you do as a professional?* | *¿Qué clase de trabajo hizo usted como un profesional?* |

Possible responses to the preceding question may include the following:

| *I was:* | *Fui:* |
| *I am:* | *Soy:* |

an accountant	*un contador*
an artist	*un artista*
an architect	*un arquitecto*
an attorney	*un abogado*
a banker	*un banquero*
a biologist	*una bióloga*
a computer programmer	*un programador de la computadora*
a computer operator	*un operador de la computadora*
a contractor	*un contratista*
an engineer	*una ingeniera*
a nurse	*una enfermera*
a physical therapist	*un terapeuta físico*
a secretary	*una secretaria*
a teacher	*un maestro*
a technician	*un técnico*

> **note** The translation for *artista* (which means "artist") deviates from the gender rule that says that nouns ending in the letter A are feminine. *Artista* applies to both the male and female genders.

Conversations About Sports

There's more to life than work! In this section of the chapter, you study sentences that describe active and passive (or spectator) sports—those sports in which we participate and those we simply watch. Some of the Spanish sports terms aren't translated, but are derived from associated English sport terms. An example of this is *fútbol*, which is derived from "football." You will hear the pronunciation of this word when you access the audio for the following sentences.

> Chapter 1, "The Rules—Short and Sweet," discusses hybrid Spanish/English terms also referred to as "Spanglish," and how the list of these terms continues to grow. The term *fútbol* is just one of many that have become part of the Spanish language.

>
> Go to audio file 06g Recreation—active sports.

Participating in Sports

We all like to talk about how good we are at whatever sport we get involved with. We sometimes do it in the hope that someone might say that we look like we have lost a pound or two. Here are a few introductory phrases followed by a list of terms for sports activities:

I enjoy playing:	Me gusta jugar:
I played:	Jugué:
baseball.	al béisbol.
football.	al fútbol americano.
soccer.	al fútbol.
basketball.	al baloncesto.
tennis.	al tenis.
billiards.	al billar.
ping pong.	al tenis de mesa.

The following two examples show you how you can change the previous sentences into questions (using the *interrogative tense*):

Do you like to play baseball?	¿Te gusta jugar al béisbol?
Do you want to play football?	¿Quieres jugar al fútbol?

Discussing Spectator Sports

Spectator sports are those that we watch in person or on television. Below are two phrases that include a blank space (...) where you can insert the applicable sports activity from the "Participating in Sports" section earlier in this chapter. The preposition *al* that precedes the preceding sports activities should be removed. The phrases are followed by two complete sentences to illustrate how the sentences should read, and one question on watching soccer.

> Go to audio file 06h
> Recreation—spectator
> sports.
>
> Listen Up   G

I like watching ...on TV.	Me gusta mirar ... en la tele.
I like watching ...in person.	Me gusta mirar ... en persona.
I like watching soccer on TV.	Me gusta mirar fútbol en la tele.
I like watching baseball in person.	Me gusta mirar béisbol en persona.
Do you enjoy watching soccer?	¿Te gusta mirar fútbol?

FOOTBALL AND SOCCER

Latin Americans refer to "soccer" as "football," or *fútbol*. To distinguish it from the football played in the U.S. they call the game played in the United States American football, or *fútbol americano*. There is no comparison between the popularity of these two sports. Football is played mainly in the U.S., but soccer is the most popular game played in most of Latin America, Europe, and Australia. In the U.S. you cannot turn to a Spanish TV channel without seeing *fútbol* being played, or highlights of some game being televised.

Other Activities of Daily Life

There is a never-ending list of things we have to do after we get out of work, or on the weekend. It is not all bad. Some of the weekend activity can help us unwind. Fortunately, in today's environment, many businesses are open late at night. The sentences you learn here can be used to have casual conversation about some of these activities.

]Go to audio file 06i After-work activities.

What are you going to do after work?	*¿Qué vas a hacer después del trabajo?*
I am going:	*Voy:*
to go to the dry cleaners.	*a ir a los tintoreros.*
to go to the mall.	*a ir al centro comercial.*
to go to the bookstore.	*a ir a la librería.*
to go to the dentist's office.	*a ir a la oficina del dentista.*
to go to a parent-teacher meeting.	*a ir a una reunión de padres y maestros.*
What are you going to do tomorrow?	*¿Qué vas a hacer mañana?*
I am going:	*Voy:*
to go to my child's school play.	*a ir para la obra teatral de la escuela de mi niño.*
to go to a birthday party.	*a ir a una fiesta de cumpleaños.*
to wash my car.	*a lavar mi coche.*
to go get an oil change.	*a ir por un cambio de aceite.*
to give my dog a bath.	*a darle un baño a mi perro.*

What are you going to do this weekend?	¿Qué vas a hacer este fin de semana?
I am going:	Voy:
to go on a trip to the mountains.	a ir de viaje a las montañas.
to visit my mother.	a visitar a mi madre.
to the beauty salon.	al salón de belleza.
to play golf.	a jugar al golf.
to read a book.	a leer un libro.
to take my children to the movies.	a llevar a mis niños al cine.
to clean my garage.	a limpiar mi garaje.
to clean house.	a limpiar la casa.
to just rest.	a simplemente descansar.

Summary

This chapter provided you with translated material that you can use to engage in conversational Spanish about a variety of things that go on in your life. It described your workplace, and provided you a large amount of translated material you can use to converse with your peers about your job, management, and office policies. It also provided text that can be used to determine whether your Hispanic peers or employees might possess experience that will better meet your company's workforce needs.

Thank goodness life is not all about work. We are able to engage in activities that allow us to recharge our batteries. This chapter provided a discussion of sports activities we can participate in or simply watch. It closed with a description of other activities that we get involved in after work.

The next chapter will provide you translated text that you can use to converse about how you spend your money. It provides a considerable number of translated words and sentences related to general shopping and shopping for groceries.

Audio Files

- ❏ 07a The parking
- ❏ 07b Store signs
- ❏ 07c Talking to sales clerks
- ❏ 07d Shopping for groceries
- ❏ 07e Domestic help shopping
- ❏ 07f Casual conversation
- ❏ 07g Food names—fruits and vegetables
- ❏ 07h Food names—dairy, spices, and canned foods
- ❏ 07i Food names—beverages, meat, and miscellaneous
- ❏ 07j Following recipes
- ❏ 07k Shopping at a *mercado*

In this chapter:

- ✳ Describing the parking lot
- ✳ Shopping in general
- ✳ Reading the store signs
- ✳ Exchanging talk with the sales staff
- ✳ Discussing grocery shopping
- ✳ Listing the food items
- ✳ Following recipes
- ✳ Shopping at a *mercado*

Shopping

Shopping is a topic that is great for making casual conversation. Everybody likes to talk about the great deal they got, or how their last purchase was a "steal," Where it may be fun to talk about shopping, it is often not too much fun to go shopping. If you go shopping for groceries or other merchandise, you might have to drive around for a long time to find a parking space. When you find one, you might have to fight for it and then walk a long way to get to the shops. Once in the store, you have to jockey among the crowds and keep from knocking over a stack of merchandise. This issue becomes a real problem during holidays and sales, when stores jam everything they can into already crowded aisles.

You can imagine what this experience may be like for people who come to the United States from a small town in some Latin American country where they do not have large super-shopping centers and malls. Discussing their experiences and reactions to the shopping "scene" in the United States can give you and your

Spanish-speaking companions a great opportunity to learn more about each other and each other's cultures. (You might learn more about *your* culture, too!)

This chapter will allow you to participate in casual conversation about shopping, and will help you understand Spanish terms used to describe shopping for groceries and other merchandise. It provides an extensive list of grocery items that you can use either to purchase or to direct others to purchase for you. This chapter also teaches you about the units of measure used in Hispanic recipes. The chapter ends with material you can use to have the shopping experience of your life—shopping at a Mexican mercado.

The Parking Lot

The ability to find a parking space at a grocery store, minimarket, or supermarket will often determine what kind of a shopping experience we have. There is the seemingly never-ending traffic. It appears that everybody chooses to go shopping when we do. If you are preparing your

Go to audio file 07a The parking lot.

Hispanic companion for this part of the shopping experience, or simply talking with him about it afterward, you need to know some key terms, phrases, and expressions used to describe the process. Here are a few sentences that can be used to talk about finding a parking space at the store, market, or mall.

Does the store have adequate parking?	*¿Tiene la tienda estacionamiento adecuado?*
Yes, it does.	*Sí, tiene.*
No, it doesn't.	*No, no tiene.*
The parking lot is very small.	*El estacionamiento es muy pequeño.*
The parking lot is congested.	*El estacionamiento está congestionado.*
The parking lot is usually empty.	*El estacionamiento está vacío usualmente.*
The parking lot is adequate.	*El estacionamiento está adecuado.*
Does the market have handicap parking?	*¿Tiene el mercado estacionamiento para el incapacitado?*
Is the parking lot lit at night?	*¿Está iluminado el estacionamiento por la noche?*
The parking lot is lit at night.	*El estacionamiento está iluminado por la noche.*
The parking lot is not lit at night.	*El estacionamiento no está iluminado por la noche.*

The parking lot does not have adequate lighting at night.	*El estacionamiento no tiene iluminación adecuada por la noche.*
It is a long walk from the parking lot to the store.	*Es una caminata del estacionamiento para la tienda.*
There are shopping carts all over the parking lot.	*Hay carretas de compras por todo el estacionamiento.*
Do they have security in the parking lot?	*¿Tienen seguridad en el estacionamiento?*
They do have security patrols in the parking lot.	*Tienen patrullas de seguridad en el estacionamiento.*
They do not have security at that store.	*No tienen seguridad en esa tienda.*

General Shopping

Though you may go grocery shopping often, you can expect to have many other shopping experiences, as well. In this section, you learn words and sentences you'll use often in general conversations about all types of shopping.

note This section doesn't include terms for major appliances or furniture; those terms are presented in Chapter 5, "Talking about Your Home and Personal Belongings."

Speaking of...

Store Signs

As you walk up to a store you may see the following signs on the building, window, or door. The name of the store, such as "Smith's" market, is not translated.

Go to audio file 07b Store signs.

Listen Up

Open	*Abierto*
Closed	*Cerrado*
Liquidation sale	*La venta de liquidación*
Inventory reduction sale	*La venta de reducción de inventario*
End of year sale	*La venta de fin de año*
Exit	*Salida*
Emergency exit	*La salida de emergencia*

HOW TO SAY LUNCH IN SPANISH

There are three words used for "lunch" in Spanish. All three are shown here. The third translation for lunch, *lonche*, is commonly used in the Southwestern United States and Mexico.

Closed for lunch	*Cerrado para almuerzo*
Closed for lunch	*Cerrado para comida*
Closed for lunch	*Cerrado para lonche*

Interaction with a Sales Clerk

A salesclerk may approach and after a friendly greeting may ask if they can help you. This section will teach you how to understand what they say, and how to respond in Spanish. You may want to review the greetings in Chapter 3, "Getting to Know One Another."

Go to audio file 07c Talking to sales clerks.

If a salesclerk does not come to assist you, you can ask:

Can someone help me?	*¿Me puede ayudar alguien?*
Can you help me?	*¿Me puede ayudar usted?*
I need help over here.	*Necesito ayuda acá.*

When the salesperson comes to assist you, he or she may ask:

May I help you?	*¿Le puedo ayudar?*
May I assist you?	*¿Le puedo asistir?*
Can I help you find something?	*¿Le puedo ayudar a encontrar algo?*

Potential responses to the salesclerk's offer to help are:

Yes, please.	*Sí, por favor.*
No, thank you.	*No, gracias.*
I am just looking around.	*Estoy mirando solamente.*
Where are your dairy products?	*¿Dónde están sus productos lácteos?*
They are on the left side of the store.	*Están en el lado izquierdo de la tienda.*
I am looking for fresh fruit.	*Busco fruta fresca.*
We received fresh mangos today.	*Recibimos mangos frescos hoy.*

Where can I find the baking spices?

¿Dónde puedo hallar las especias de hornear?

> Follow me and I will show you where.

> Sígame y le mostraré donde.

Where is the dishwashing detergent?

¿Dónde está el detergente de lavar los platos?

> It is in aisle five.

> Está en el pasillo cinco.

I'm looking for a shirt.

Busco una camisa.

I want to buy some pants.

Quiero comprar unos pantalones.

I want to buy a dress.

Quiero comprar un vestido.

I want to buy shoes.

Quiero comprar zapatos.

What size do you wear?

¿Qué tamaño calza usted?

> My neck size is 16 inches.

> El tamaño de mi cuello es dieciséis pulgadas.

> My sleeve size is 35 inches.

> El tamaño de mi manga es treinta y cinco pulgadas.

> I have a 32-inch waist.

> Tengo una cintura de treinta y dos pulgadas.

> My dress size is 8.

> El tamaño de mi vestido es ocho.

> My shoe size is 7.

> El tamaño de mi zapato es siete.

SHOE SIZES

The U.S. and Mexico have different shoe sizes. Men's U.S. shoe sizes are 1 1/2 inches larger than those in Mexico. Women's U.S. shoes sizes are 3 inches larger that those in Mexico. A U.S. size 9 men's shoe is a size 7 1/2 in Mexico. A U.S. size 8 women's shoe is a size 5 in Mexico.

If you find something you are interested in or would like to try it on, you can ask:

> How much does this cost?   ¿Cuánto cuesta esto?

The response will be a dollar amount. Here is an example.

> It costs $19.95.

> Cuesta diecinueve dólares y noventa y cinco centavos.

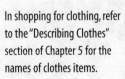

In shopping for clothing, refer to the "Describing Clothes" section of Chapter 5 for the names of clothes items.

Here are some sentences you can use to discuss prices:

| Is it on sale? | ¿Está a la venta? |
| Isn't it on sale? | ¿No está a la venta? |

note You can find Spanish terms for dollar amounts in Chapter 2, "Letters, Numbers, Dates, and Dollars."

To these questions, the merchant might respond like this:

| That is the sale price. | Ése es el precio de venta. |

If you're bargaining, you might ask the merchant this question:

| Is that the best price you can give me? | ¿Eso es el mejor precio que usted me puede dar? |

The merchant response to that question might one of these sentences:

| That is the best price I can give you. | Ése es el mejor precio que le puedo dar. |
| Ok, I'll let you have it for $16.50. | Está bien, se lo vendo por dieciséis dólares y cincuenta centavos. |

note Learn more about bargaining in a Mexican market or *mercado* in "Shopping at a *Mercado*," later in this chapter.

The following is a collection of other questions and declarations you may be able to use in your shopping.

Do you have something cheaper?	¿Tiene usted algo más barato?
Can I try it on?	¿Me lo puedo probar?
Where are the fitting rooms?	¿Dónde están los cuartos de pruebas?
I want to buy it.	Quiero comprarlo.
I would like to buy it.	Me gustaría comprarlo.
I want to pay for it.	Quiero pagar por él.
Where do I pay?	¿Dónde pago?
I'm going to pay cash.	Voy a pagar al contado.
Do you accept credit cards?	¿Acepta usted tarjetas de crédito?
Do you accept...? (name of credit card)	¿Acepta usted...?
Can I return it, if I change my mind?	¿Lo puedo devolver, si cambio mi mente?
I don't want to buy it.	No quiero comprarlo.
It is too expensive.	Es demasiado caro.

I am looking for a better price.	*Ando buscando un mejor precio.*
I want to look around some more.	*Quiero seguir buscando.*
I don't like the color.	*No me gusta el color.*
I don't like the pattern.	*No me gusta el diseño.*
It doesn't fit me.	*No me queda bien.*
I am looking for better quality.	*Ando buscando mejor calidad.*

Shopping for Groceries

We purchase food items more often than any-thing else. We buy food items at the grocery store and when we place an order for a meal at a restaurant. In this section, you learn phrases and sentences you'll use to discuss shopping for groceries at a market or grocery store. Chapter 8,

Go to audio file 07d Shopping for groceries.

"Eating Out," will teach you the names of the food items that are used to prepare a meal. This section will guide you through the process of stating where you shop or have shopped, and will allow you to inquire about where to locate certain kinds of stores.

I shop for groceries at:	*Compro abarrotes en:*
I went to:	*Fui a:*
I went to buy groceries at:	*Fui para comprar abarrotes en:*
the grocery store.	*la tienda de comestibles.*
the market.	*el mercado.*
the minimarket.	*el minimercado.*
the supermarket.	*el supermercado.*
Where is:	*¿Dónde está:*
Where can I find:	*¿Dónde puedo encontrar:*

In addition to the store names you learned earlier, you can use any of these store names to complete the preceding questions:

the meat market?	*el mercado de la carne?*
the butcher shop?	*la carnicería?*
the bakery?	*la panadería?*
I need to buy the	*Necesito comprar los*
ingredients for a recipe.	*ingredientes para una receta.*

I have to buy groceries for a dinner I am preparing.	*Tengo que comprar abarrotes para una cena que preparo.*

Domestic Help and Grocery Shopping

If you have a Hispanic domestic worker who helps prepare your meals, you need to be able to talk to them about grocery shopping. Here are some sentences you can use to ask them to go to the store for you.

Go to audio file 07e Domestic help shopping.

I need for you to go to the store for me.	*Necesito que usted vaya a la tienda para mí.*
Will you go to the store for me?	*¿Quieres ir a la tienda para mí?*
Please go to the store for me.	*Por favor vaya a la tienda para mí.*
You buy what you need to prepare our meals for the week.	*Usted compre lo que usted necesita para preparar nuestras comidas para la semana.*
Here is a list of what I want you to buy:	*Aquí está una lista de lo que yo quiero que usted compre:*

You may want to try to prepare the grocery list in Spanish using the translated grocery items listed in the section titled "Food Item Names," later in this chapter.

Casual Conversation About Grocery Shopping

If you just want to make conversation about grocery shopping, or a specific store, here are some comments that can be used:

Go to audio file 07f Casual conversation.

I like to go shopping for groceries.	*Me gusta ir de compras por abarrotes.*
I do not like to go shopping for groceries.	*No me gusta ir a comprar abarrotes.*
Do you like shopping for groceries?	*¿Le gusta ir a comprar abarrotes?*
I make a list of things I need to buy.	*Hago una lista de cosas que necesito comprar.*
I save money with coupons.	*Ahorro dinero con cupones.*
I shop when there is a sale.	*Voy de compras cuando hay una venta.*
I like stores with wide aisles.	*Me gustan las tiendas con pasillos anchos.*
I like stores that are clean.	*Me gustan las tiendas que están limpias.*

Food Item Names

The food items listed here can be appended to the phrases that this section starts out with. These phrases can be applied to other food items not in the following list that you may find in some Spanish dictionary, such as a can of tuna.

Go to audio file 07g Food names—fruits and vegetables.

When talking about any of the food items you learn here, you can use the following four introductory phrases:

I need to buy:	*Necesito comprar:*
I am going to buy:	*Voy a comprar:*
I bought:	*Compré:*
My recipe requires:	*Mi receta requiere:*

Fruits and vegetables

Use the phrases that follow to talk about fruit:

six apples.	*seis manzanas.*
a couple of pounds of bananas.	*dos libras de bananos.*
a small bunch of plantains.	*un racimo pequeño de plátanos.*

THE BANANA IN LATIN AMERICA

Talking Points

The banana grows profusely in the tropics. The term banana is pronounced the same in Spanish as in English. It is often pronounced with the male gender, or *banano*, as in the first translation of this word. The banana comes in another form that's less common in the U.S., called a "plantain" *(plátano)*. The plantain is a smaller banana, high in starch, and not sweet like the banana we are used to until it is nearly over-ripe. Plantain is cooked and used in Latin American meals in ways similar to the way potatoes are used in other parts of the world.

a fresh cantaloupe.	*un melón fresco.*
a box of cherries.	*una caja de cerezas.*
a couple of figs.	*dos higos.*
some grapefruits.	*unas toronjas.*
three lemons.	*tres limones.*

four limes.	cuatro limas.
a honeydew melon.	un melón de pulpa verdosa.
three to four oranges.	de tres a cuatro naranjas.
some peaches.	unos duraznos.
a pound of pears.	una libra de peras.
a pineapple.	una piña.
a plum.	una ciruela.
a few raspberries.	unas frambuesas.
a small basket of strawberries.	una canasta pequeña de unas fresas.

Here are the names of some popular vegetables:

Vegetables:	Los vegetales:
two avocados.	dos aguacates.
a pound of beans.	una libra de frijoles.
a head of cabbage.	un col.
a bundle of carrots.	un atado de zanahorias.
a cauliflower.	una coliflor.
some celery.	un apio.

TALKING ABOUT CHILES

The Spanish word for chili pepper, or chili is *chile*. Chiles are important components in authentic Hispanic cuisine.

a sack of chili.	un costal de chile.
red pepper.	el pimiento rojo.
crushed red chili.	el chile colorado triturado.
green chili.	el chile verde.
chopped chili.	el chile picado.
chopped green chili.	el chile verde picado.
whole green chili.	el chile verde entero.

a quarter-pound of chili peppers.	*un cuarto de libra de chile.*
a pound of jalapeño chili peppers.	*una libra de chile jalapeño.*
a lettuce.	*una lechuga.*
a package of mushrooms.	*un paquete de champiñones.*
one-half kilo of onions.	*un medio kilo de cebollas.*
chives.	*los cebollinos.*
a half-dozen ears of corn.	*una media docena de mazorcas.*
a cucumber.	*un pepino.*
an onion.	*una cebolla.*
chopped prickly pear.	*el nopal cortado en trocitos.*

NOPALITOS
–A DELICACY

The prickly pear or *nopal*, a flat round cactus about the size of a pancake, can be found in the deserts of the Southwestern U.S., and northern Mexico. It is a mean cactus that can cause a lot of damage to an unwary hiker. The nopal is full of spines, some large and some very small. The small ones can attach to your skin simply by your touching them. They cause a lot of pain and are very difficult to see and pull out. Mexicans remove the spines and boil or fry the nopal. When boiled the nopal tastes a little like boiled asparagus. I have seen people prepare something similar to an egg omelet by frying the nopal with egg and condiments of choice. Once prepared, the mean nopal becomes a delicious *nopalitos* plate.

brussel sprouts.	*el col de brusela.*
a sack of potatoes.	*un costal de papas.*
sweet potatoes.	*los camotes.*
a small bunch of radishes.	*un racimo pequeño de rábanos.*
a packet of four-tomatoes.	*un paquete de cuatro tomates.*
vegetables.	*unas legumbres.*
a vegetable salad in a package.	*una ensalada de vegetales en un paquete.*

Dairy products, Spices, and Packaged Food

Use the following phrases to talk about dairy products, spices you use for baking, and a wide range of packaged foods:

Go to audio file 07h Food names—dairy, spices, and canned foods.

I want to buy:	*Quiero comprar:*
Dairy products:	*Los productos lácteos:*
four hundred twenty-five grams of butter.	cuatrocientos veinticinco gramos de mantequilla.
one pound of cheese.	una libra de queso.
a package of cream cheese.	un paquete de queso de crema.
a gallon of ice cream.	un galón de helado.
a pint of 2% milk.	una pinta de leche de dos por ciento.
a quart of skim milk.	un cuarto de galón de leche desnatada.
a half-gallon of milk.	un medio galón de leche.
one gallon of chocolate milk.	un galón de leche de chocolate.
sour cream.	la crema agria.
Spices:	*Las Especias:*
anise.	el anís.
cinnamon.	la canela.
a package of ground cloves.	un paquete de clavos de especia molidos.
cumin.	el comino.
a clove of garlic.	un diente de ajo.
nutmeg.	la nuez moscada.
oregano.	el orégano.
extra-fine paprika.	la paprika extrafina.
parsley.	el perejil.
a can of pepper.	una lata de pimienta.
sage.	la salvia.
salt.	la sal.
some thyme.	un tomillo.
vanilla.	la vainilla.
Cans, jars, and bottles:	*Latas, tarros y botellas:*
a can of beans.	una lata de frijoles.
a can of cranberry sauce.	una lata de salsa de arándanos.

a bottle of cooking oil.	*una botella de aceite de cocinar.*
a bottle of ketchup.	*una botella de salsa de tomate.*
one-half liter of lemonade.	*un medio litro de limonada.*
five cans of peas.	*cinco latas de chícharos.*
three cans of soup.	*tres latas de caldo.*
a can of vegetable stew.	*una lata de potaje de verduras.*
a jar of mayonnaise.	*un tarro de mayonesa.*
a jar of mustard.	*un tarro de mostaza.*
vegetable oil.	*el aceite vegetal.*
a jar of peanut butter.	*un tarro de mantequilla de maní.*
four cans of peas.	*cuatro latas de guisantes.*
a bottle of vinegar.	*una botella de vinagre.*

Beverages, Meat, Dried Products, and Miscellaneous Food Items

Use the following two introductory phrases, or any of the introductory phrases in the preceding two sections to discuss the food items in this section.

Go to audio file 07i Food names—beverages, meat, and miscellaneous.

I want to have a cookout and I need to buy:	*Quiero tener una comida al aire libre y necesito comprar:*
I invited friends for dinner and need to buy:	*Invité a amigos para cenar y necesito comprar:*
Coffee, tea, and soft drinks:	*El café, el té, y los refrescos:*
apple juice	*el jugo de manzana.*
decaffeinated coffee.	*el café descafeinado.*
a pound of coffee.	*una libra de café.*
instant coffee.	*el café instantáneo.*
a liter of cola.	*un litro de kola.*
a half-gallon of orange juice.	*un medio galón de jugo de naranja.*
some tea.	*un té.*
bottled water.	*el agua embotellada.*
a dozen bottles of mineral water.	*una docena de botellas de agua mineral.*

Meat products:	Los productos de carne:
two pounds of ground beef.	dos libras de carne molida.
a round steak.	un bistec de rueda.
a couple of T-bone steaks.	dos chuletas en forma de T.
a package of bologna.	un paquete de salchicha.
a package of thin sliced ham.	un paquete de jamón cortado en tajadas finas.
one kilo of bacon.	un kilo de tocino.
some pork chops.	unas chuletas de cerdo.
a pound of pork ribs.	una libra de costillas de carne de cerdo.
pork sausage.	la salchicha de carne de cerdo.
four fish fillets.	cuatro filetes de pescado.
a lobster tail.	una cola de langosta.
a pound of trout.	una libra de trucha.
a chicken.	un pollo.
chicken breast.	la pechuga de pollo.
a small turkey.	un pavo pequeño.
a package of smoked turkey.	un paquete de pavo ahumado.
Dried foods:	Las comidas secadas:
a bag of rice.	una bolsa de arroz.
a box of stuffing.	una caja de relleno.
a box of macaroni and cheese.	un caja de macarrones con queso.
a box of corn flakes.	una caja de hojuelas de maíz.
Miscellaneous Products:	Los productos diversos:
a box of baking soda.	una caja de polvo de hornear.
a box of cereal.	una caja de cereal frío.
instant oatmeal.	la avena de cereal instantánea.
a dozen doughnuts.	una docena de donas.
a box of cookies.	una caja de galletas.
one dozen eggs.	una docena de huevos.
horseradish.	el rábano picante.
a bag of peanuts (Latin America).	una bolsa de maní.
a kilo of peanuts (Mexico).	un kilo de cacahuates.

a pie.	un pastel.
a pizza.	una pizza.
a pumpkin pie.	un pastel de calabaza.
a gallon of sherbet.	un galón de sorbete.
some spaghetti sauce.	una salsa del espagueti.
a pound of granulated sugar.	una libra de azúcar granulada.
a box of low-calorie sugar.	una caja de azúcar baja en calorías.
ten pounds of flour.	diez libras de harina.
a box of tea bags.	una caja de bolsitas de té.

Following Recipes

The "Shopping for Groceries" section includes many of the ingredients found in recipes. Units of measure for recipes can be found in Chapter 2. It is not possible to present a list of translated recipes. Most recipes are someone's creation, and they may have copyrights to them. One thing that can be done is to include a series of action words and phrases found in recipes.

Go to audio file 07j
Following recipes.

Pour it into:	Échalo en:
Chop and throw it into:	Pícalo en trocitos y échalo en:
Crush and sprinkle into:	Tritura y salpica en:
Mix it into:	Combínalo en:
Stir and put it in:	Revuélvelo y ponlo en:
Place it in:	Deposítalo en:
a small frying pan.	un sartén pequeño.
a medium-sized frying pan.	un sartén tamaño mediano.
a large frying pan.	un sartén grande.
a bowl.	un tazón.
a mixing bowl.	una batidora.
a cup.	una taza.
a saucer.	un platillo.
a blender.	una licuadora.

Once you have placed the ingredients into a processing unit, the next action is to do something to ensure its proper cooking. The following words and phrases address some of the action. Insert the item, for example, chicken, following the action phrase.

Stir the ingredients gently.	*Revuelve los ingredientes suavemente.*
Stir the pot briskly.	*Revuelve la olla enérgicamente.*
Scramble it.	*Bátelo.*
Deep fry…	*Fríe por inmersión en aceite…*
Deep fry in hot oil…	*Fríe por inmersión en aceite caliente…*
Grill…	*Asa a la parrilla…*
Roast…	*Asa…*
Bake…	*Hornea…*
Cook…	*Cocina…*
Dice…	*Pica en cúbitos…*
Spread some butter on…	*Unta mantequilla en…*
Let it simmer.	*Déjalo hervir a fuego lento.*
Cut…	*Corta…*
Slice…	*Parte en rebanadas…*
Boil…	*Hierve…*
Refrigerate…	*Refrigera…*
Freeze…	*Congela…*
Sauté…	*Sofríe en una cazuela abierta…*
Smother with…	*Cubre con…*
Serve…	*Sirve…*
Set the oven at 400 degrees.	*Pon el horno a cuatrocientos grados.*
Cook it for 45 minutes.	*Cuécelo por cuarenta y cinco minutos.*

The following recipe on how to make corn bread is provided to give you an idea on how the phrases in this section can be used to understand a Spanish recipe, or talk about how to prepare a dish.

Corn Bread	*El Pan De Maíz*
1 egg	*un huevo*
2 cups buttermilk	*dos tazas de suero de la leche*
1 cup water	*una taza de agua*
1 teaspoon baking soda	*una cucharita de bicarbonato de soda*
2 teaspoons salt	*dos cucharitas de sal*
corn meal	*la harina de maíz*

Combine egg, buttermilk, and water;	Combine el huevo, el suero de la leche, y el agua;
Add salt and soda.	Añada sal y soda.
Pour corn meal into the bowl.	Eche la harina de maíz en el tazón.
Stir until you have cake batter consistency.	Revuélvalo hasta que tenga la consistencia de pasta de pastel.
Bake at 500 degrees for 15 to 20 minutes in a well-greased 10-inch pan.	Hornéelo a quinientos grados por quince a veinte minutos en una tartera de diez pulgadas bien engrasada.

Shopping at a *Mercado*

Shopping at a Mexican market or *mercado* can be an interesting experience. The Mexican *mercado* offers a variety of handicrafts, artwork, and clothing. They sell pottery, figurines, silver, pewter, Mexican blankets called *serapes*, ponchos, leather belts, purses, wallets, baskets, onyx, jewelry, paintings, embroidered dresses, and trinkets. They sell all kinds of foodstuff, including fast-food and a large array of vegetables and fruits. You can even purchase knock-off imitations of expensive wristwatches for under $50. As you walk into the Mexican *mercado,* you will discover that it has many merchants selling their wares in individual stalls. Some sell the same or similar items. Many of these same wares are sold at stores outside the *mercado*.

MEXICAN PIÑATAS

One of the children's favorite playthings is the *piñata*, and you can find these for sale in many Mexican *mercados*. A *piñata* is made out of newspaper and glue with a hollow inside. It is molded into almost any shape desired, preferably a favorite animal, and covered on the outside with colorful tissue paper. Mexican families traditionally celebrate children's birthdays with a piñata. They fill the piñata with wrapped candy and other goodies. They blindfold the children and have them take turns at trying to break the piñata with a stick. When the piñata is broken, the children scramble to get to the candy that falls to the ground.

Bargaining for the Best Price

One of the great things about shopping anywhere is the feeling that you got a bargain. We
do not get the opportunity to barter in stores in
the U.S. Make your visit to the Mexican *mercado*
more enjoyable by planning to barter. You can
and should barter at the mercado. Never pay the
price on the price tag. There is a tremendous
markup on prices, and the shopkeepers are
always willing to negotiate. The best way to get
the shopkeeper to reduce the price is to pretend
that you are not interested in buying the particular item at the stated price. Even if you are dying
to purchase the item, put on your best act to convince the shopkeeper you are not interested.
Walk away. The shopkeeper will follow you, and
you will be amazed at how much the price will
drop before you walk out the door.

Go to audio file 07k Shopping
at a mercado.

tip   As you walk in, you will get the
usual greeting and may even
get greeted in English.
Shopkeepers are not ashamed to try out, or
maybe show off their English on you.

You should always get price quotes in U.S.
currency. You know the value of the U.S. currency, and it eliminates the potential for
overcharging you on the exchange rate.

The material provided here for you to use in bargaining can be applied to shopping
at a *mercado*, or stores outside the *mercado*.

If you see an item you are interested in, pick it up or point it out and ask or say:

What is the price on this?	*¿Qué precio tiene esto?*
How much do you want for this?	*¿Cuánto quiere usted por esto?*
Give me the best price and I will buy it.	*Deme el mejor precio y lo compro.*

The response may be a price quote ($20.95 is used as an example):

Twenty dollars and 95 cents.	*Veinte dólares y noventa y cinco centavos.*

Other responses may be:

I'll let you have it for…	*Se lo vendo por…*

(The merchant will give a price quote.)

If you do not like the price quoted, and if you have not priced the item elsewhere,
you can say:

Not good enough.	*No es aceptable.*
That is too much money.	*Eso es demasiado dinero.*
The price is too high.	*El precio es demasiado alto.*

That is more than I want to pay for it.	Eso es más de lo que quiero pagar.
I'm sure I can get it cheaper at another store.	Estoy seguro que lo puedo obtener más barato en otra tienda.
No, thanks.	No, gracias.

The merchant's response may be:

That is the lowest price I can offer.	Ése es el precio mínimo que puedo ofrecer.
I am giving you the lowest price.	Le doy el precio mínimo.
I am giving you the discount price.	Le doy el precio con descuento.
I am almost giving it to you free!	¡Casi se lo doy gratis!
That is the sale price today.	Ése es el precio de la mercadería en rebaja hoy.
Okay, I'll let you have it for:	Está bien, se lo vendo por:

The merchant may simply state the following specifying a certain price:

Give me…	Deme…

THE ART OF BARGAINING

I am not going to encourage you to lie, but you can take advantage of certain shopping techniques that will result in lower prices. In bargaining for a lower price, if you have already been offered a lower price at another stall or store, state that. The "lower price" may have been only $1 lower. You do not have to divulge how much lower the price was at another store. You simply want to convey the information that you have been offered a better deal elsewhere. That should result in a price reduction in the item you are trying to buy. You should try to negotiate a lower price only if you are serious about buying something. Merchants take offense when they suspect that you are bargaining just for the fun of it, and not serious about buying anything.

I have received a better price elsewhere.	He recibido un mejor precio en otro sitio.
I can buy it at another stall for less.	Lo puedo comprar en otro puesto por menos.
I can buy it at another store for less.	Lo puedo comprar en otra tienda por menos.
The market across the street offered it for… (applicable dollars and cents)	El mercado al otro lado de la calle me lo ofreció por…

Finalizing Your Purchase and Making Returns

Check everything you intend to buy before you pay for it. Try to get a receipt for anything you purchase, in the event that you have to return the article. If there is anything wrong with any of your purchases, or if you change your mind about anything you purchased, you may wish to return them. You can use the following statements to state why you wish to return an item.

I wish to return this item because:	*Deseo devolver este artículo porque:*
it is broken.	está quebrado.
it does not work.	no funciona.
it is torn.	está roto.
it has a split seam.	está descosido.
it is defective.	Está defectuoso.
I didn't like it.	no me gustó.

Summary

In this chapter you were provided translated text with audio for every aspect of your shopping experience. You learned to talk about the parking lot, and how to read store signs. You also learned how to talk to a Spanish-speaking sales clerk, and how to tell your Hispanic domestic worker what groceries to buy for you. You were provided an extensive list of translated food names, and how you can work with them in a recipe. You were provided material that will allow you to have a very interesting experience as you shop in a Mexican market, or *mercado*. This chapter taught you how to bargain for the best price on Mexican products and souvenirs. Even if you don't buy anything, you will enjoy haggling with the merchants on the price. If they give you a rock-bottom price on an item, and you don't buy it, they will be mumbling things that it's best we don't translate.

In the next chapter we are going to teach you how to apply your newly learned ability to speak Spanish at a Hispanic restaurant. We will guide you through steps to find a good restaurant, make reservations, and go there for breakfast, lunch, or dinner. You will learn how to read a menu, place an order, and pay for your meal. If something does not meet your expectations, we will teach you how to bring that up to the manager's attention. The restaurant, in preparation of your meal, uses many of the food ingredients discussed in this chapter. We will try not to repeat those items in the next chapter. Instead we will provide you the Spanish words for the main entree and side dishes that include the food items presented in this chapter.

8

Eating Out

Hispanic restaurants are no longer confined to the Southwestern United States. They are popping up all over the place. If you are not patronizing those restaurants because you don't know the language, you are missing out on one of the most pleasant adventures in life.

The material in this chapter will help you use your Spanish language skills to place an order or request other services at a restaurant. It will also help you understand and participate in restaurant talk if you ever come across it. Most Hispanic restaurants have a bilingual menu. A lot of the smaller places, especially the fast food eateries, have their menu posted on the wall. The menu may contain the names of ethnic food, such as *Enchiladas*, or *Ropa Vieja*, which literally means "old clothes." The latter is a delicious plate of shredded beef with its origins in Cuba. I got a chance to taste it in Panama City, Panama. The waitress had to do a lot of talking to convince me to try it, but I was glad I did.

The terms and phrases shown in this chapter can be used to discuss any subject having to do with a

Hispanic restaurant. Hispanics will understand all of the translated text in this chapter. Some of the terms that may not be understood by all Hispanics are menu item names that are unique to a specific Latin American country. There is no translation or English counterpart for many of these ethnic menu items. Upscale restaurants will sometimes provide a brief description of the menu items.

You'll also learn how to find the restaurant, read the menus, inquire about ingredients, and order and pay for menu items. Finally, you learn how to ask for special types of assistance while dining out, such as finding the restroom or requesting medical attention.

Finding a Restaurant

I'm sure you've heard the old saying that if you want to find good food when on the road, you should ask a truck driver. They have tried all the eating places and know where the good food is served. In the same vein, if you want to know

> Go to audio file 08a Finding a restaurant.

where they serve the most authentic Hispanic food, ask a Hispanic. In the event that the Hispanic person does not speak English, the terms and expressions you learn here can help you with that.

I am looking for a restaurant that serves authentic Hispanic food.	*Busco un restaurante que sirve comida hispana auténtica.*
Do you know where they serve good Hispanic food?	*¿Sabe usted dónde se sirve buena comida hispana?*

You may want to inquire about a restaurant that specializes in food from a particular Latin American country. The following phrases show you how to ask for a restaurant that serves food from different Latin American countries.

Do you know where they serve:	*¿Sabe usted dónde se sirve:*
Mexican food?	*comida mejicana?*
Nicaraguan food?	*comida nicaragüense?*
Honduran food?	*comida hondureña?*
Puerto Rican food?	*comida puertorriqueña?*
Argentinean food?	*comida de argentina?*
Cuban food?	*comida cubana?*
Venezuelan food?	*comida venezolana?*
Paraguayan food?	*comida paraguayana?*

Peruvian food?	comida peruana?
Colombian food?	comida colombiana?
Uruguayan food?	comida uruguaya?
Chilean food?	comida chilena?
Costa Rican food?	comida costarricense?
Jamaican food?	comida jamaicana?

Possible responses are:

I don't know of any good restaurant.	No sé de ningún buen restaurante.
My family and I eat at the Restaurante de Mariscos.	Mi familia y yo comemos en el Restaurante de Mariscos.
I like to eat at the Restaurante de Mariscos.	Me gusta comer en el Restaurante de Mariscos.
I recommend the Restaurante de Mariscos.	Recomiendo el Restaurante de Mariscos.

note The word *mariscos* means seafood.

The response may indicate the country related to the food served at a particular restaurant. A couple of countries are used in the following examples.

They serve good Nicaraguan food at the Restaurante de Mariscos.	Sirven buena comida nicaragüense en el Restaurante de Mariscos.
They have exceptional Puerto Rican food at the Restaurante de Mariscos.	Tienen comida puertorriqueña excepcional en el Restaurante de Mariscos.

Making Reservations

Generally, high-class Hispanic restaurants have personnel that speak English. In the event that you were to call to make reservations and get a response by someone who does not speak English, the following translated questions and sentences will help.

Go to audio file 08b Making reservations.

Do you accept reservations?	*¿Acepta usted reservaciones?*
Do you require reservations?	*¿Requiere usted reservaciones?*

If the response is in the affirmative, then you can proceed to make the reservation. Replace the number in the party, and the time shown in the following example with the desired number and time.

I want to make reservations for two at 6:00 PM on Saturday.	*Quiero hacer reservaciones para dos el sábado a las seis de la tarde.*

SPEAKING OF NUMBERS AND TIME

Remember that you can replace the information shown as an example with the actual number, date, or time. Chapter 2, "Letters, Numbers, Dates, and Times" includes the translation for this information.

If you happen to be at a hotel where the bellman or bellhop does not speak English, and you want to inquire about the reservation policy at some restaurant or other similar establishment, you can use the following:

I would like to dine at the Restaurante de Mariscos.	*Quisiera cenar en el Restaurante de Mariscos.*
We would like to eat at the Restaurante de Mariscos.	*Quisiéramos comer en el Restaurante de Mariscos.*
Do you know if they require reservations at that restaurant?	*¿Sabe usted si requieren reservaciones en ese restaurante?*

The response will be:

Yes, they do.	*Sí, lo requieren.*
No, they do not.	*No, no lo requieren.*
I don't know.	*No sé.*

The following translations will help if you want the bellhop, bellman, or other hotel employee to make reservations for you.

Please make reservations for two people at 6:00 PM this evening.	*Por favor haga reservaciones para dos personas a las seis esta tarde.*

Conducting the Business of Dining

In this section, you learn how to use Spanish terms, phrases, and sentences to talk to the host/hostess or waiter as you walk into the restaurant. You will also learn sentences to request a menu and place an order. This section also discusses common items found on breakfast, lunch, and dinner menus in Hispanic restaurants.

Go to audio file 08c The menu.

As you walk into the restaurant, either alone or with a group, the host, hostess, waiter, or waitress will greet you. In this example we will assume that your interaction is with a waiter, called a *camarero* in Spanish.

waiter	*camarero*

After the greeting the waiter will ask:

How many in your group?	*¿Cuántos en su grupo?*

tip The information in this section is provided so you can practice engaging in the interaction that will take place between you and the waiter as you walk into a restaurant. Start out with a few simple phrases, such as "I want" or *Quiero*, memorize them, and use them the next time you go to a Hispanic restaurant. To expand on your list of memorized phrases, memorize the names of 10 food items and a couple of beverages. Practice them on Hispanics every chance you get.

Your response will be whatever number is in your group. You will find the translation of numbers in the "Numbers" section in Chapter 2.

There are five in our group.	*Hay cinco en nuestro grupo.*

The waiter will take your group to your table and give you a menu.

Follow me to your table.	*Síganme a su mesa.*
Here are your menus.	*Aquí están sus menús.*

The following phrases are useful for requesting many types of menus:

Let me see a menu, please.	*Déjeme ver un menú, por favor.*
Let me see a breakfast menu.	*Déjeme ver un menú del desayuno.*
Let me see a lunch menu.	*Déjeme ver un menú del almuerzo.*

Let me see a dinner menu.	Déjeme ver un menú de la cena.
Let me see a dessert menu.	Déjeme ver un menú del postre.
Let me see a vegetarian menu.	Déjeme ver un menú vegetariano.

When you receive the menu you've requested, you respond by thanking the server:

Thanks.	Gracias.

A common practice is for the waiter to take your beverage order while you look at the menu. For more detailed information on ordering beverages go to the "Ordering Beverages" section later in this chapter.

May I take your beverage order?	¿Puedo tomar su orden de la bebida?

Your response:

I want iced tea.	Quiero té helado.

After he delivers the beverages, he will ask if you are ready to order your meal.

How can I help you?	¿En qué puedo servirles?

The waiter records the order and proceeds to place it with the cooks. For more detailed information on how to order your meals, go to the "Placing an Order," "Ordering Breakfast Items," "Ordering Lunch and Dinner Items," "Ordering Side Dishes," and "Ordering Desserts" sections later in this chapter.

Very well, I will be back soon.	Muy bien, ya vuelvo pronto.
Here is your food.	Aquí está su comida.

Go to the "Understanding the Ingredients in Hispanic Dishes" section for a detailed list of ingredients that went into your food order.

Thanks.	Gracias.

You may discover that you need something, or simply need to bring a problem to the attention of the waiter or waitress. The best way to get their attention, if they are not within hearing distance, is to raise your hand with the index finger pointing up when they look your way. If they are within hearing distance, you call them *Joven* or *Señorita*. The waiter's or waitress's age or marital status do not matter. Calling them by these two names is considered a compliment and will get you the best results.

Young man!	¡Joven!
Miss!	¡Señorita!
There is a problem with my food.	Hay un problema con mi comida.

For detailed information on how to complain about a problem, go to the "Registering Complaints" section later in this chapter.

I am sorry.	*Lo siento.*
Please bring the check.	*Por favor traiga la cuenta.*

For detailed information on how to talk about paying your check go to the "Paying for Your Meal" section later in this chapter.

Here is your check.	*Aquí está su cuenta.*
Thank you very much.	*Muchas gracias.*
Goodbye.	*Adiós.*

Placing an Order

In placing an order for a meal, generally you select a main entrée. You then order side dishes to go along with your meal selection. In this section you are provided some phrases that you can use to make your main entrée selection. Select the phrase that applies to the menu item you want to order, then select from the food selections listed following the phrases. Instruction on how to order a side dish, drink, or dessert will be provided later in this section.

> Go to audio file 08d Ordering the main dish.

I want to order:	*Quiero ordenar:*
I would like to order:	*Quisiera ordenar:*
I need for you to bring me:	*Necesito que me traiga:*
Please bring me:	*Por favor tráigame:*

"HAM AND EGGS, PLEASE"

There is a story about a recently arrived young Mexican who tried very hard to learn how to order breakfast at a restaurant. All he knew how to order in English was "Ham and eggs, please." After a month of eating the same thing, he asked a friend to help him order something else. His friend taught him how to order "an omelet with hash browns," and since he wanted to order dessert, "a piece of pie and a glass of milk." He was excited the next morning and had a big smile as he walked into the restaurant. The waitress asked him if he wanted the same thing he always ordered, and he said no. He said "I want an omelet with hash browns and a piece of glass and a pie of milk." "What?" the waitress asked. He quickly replied, "Ham and eggs, please."

With the skills you learn in this book, you will not have this young man's problem.

Match the sample orders shown in the following sections with the appropriate phrase from the preceding list.

Ordering Breakfast Items

The following phrases are useful when placing breakfast orders:

scrambled eggs.	unos huevos batidos.
eggs sunny-side up.	unos huevos, fritos por un solo lado.
fried eggs, medium.	unos huevos fritos, mediano.
fried eggs, hard.	unos huevos fritos, duro.
ham and eggs.	unos huevos con jamón.
bacon and eggs.	unos huevos con tocino.
sausage and eggs.	unos huevos con longaniza.
egg omelette	una tortilla de huevos.
a poached egg.	un huevo escalfado.
a soft-boiled egg.	un huevo pasado por agua.
a hard-boiled egg.	un huevo duro.
a hot cereal.	un cereal caliente.
cold cereal.	el cereal frío.
pancakes.	los panqueques.

Ordering Lunch and Dinner Items

Use these phrases when placing lunch orders:

a chicken sandwich.	un emparedado de pollo.
a tuna sandwich.	un sándwich de atún.
a tuna salad.	una ensalada de atún.
a hamburger.	una hamburguesa.
a salad.	una ensalada.
a turkey and avocado sandwich.	un emparedado de pavo con aguacate.
a soup.	una sopa.

These phrases might prove useful when you are placing orders for dinner:

the fried chicken.	el pollo frito.
the grilled chicken.	el pollo a la parrilla.
an order of shrimp.	un orden de camarón.
stuffed flounder.	la platija rellena.
halibut.	el halibut.
trout.	la trucha.
the lobster tail.	la cola de langosta.
the New York steak.	el bistec de Nueva York.
the t-bone steak.	el bistec t-bone.
the breaded veal cutlet.	la chuleta de ternera empanizada.
the pork chops.	las chuletas de puerco.
spaghetti and meat balls.	el espagueti y las albóndigas.
ham.	el jamón.
roast turkey.	el pavo asado.
grilled fish.	el pez a la parrilla.

Once you order the main dish, you can order side dishes using the following phrases:

PLAYING MENU ROULETTE

Ordering from a menu written in a foreign language offers some challenges. I can remember two occasions where I ordered items from a menu without really knowing what I was ordering. These incidents seem funny now, but they were embarrassing at the time. The first is when my wife and I were traveling in Mexico. We went to a nice restaurant, studied the menu, and selected an item that seemed very interesting. I didn't want to ask the waiter what I was ordering. After all, I considered myself a *Chicano* (Mexican American). I ordered *Manitas de Cerdo*, which I thought sounded like something exotic. The waiter brought a deep plate with two pig's feet, in some kind of soup. The pig's feet wouldn't have been so bad, but they were in dire need of a shave (or perhaps a haircut). I hadn't even realized I was ordering pork; after all, how was I to know that *cerdo* means pig? We called pigs *marranos* in New Mexico where I grew up.

The second incident happened in a very fancy German restaurant that had its walls lined with beautiful artwork, in Baltimore, MD. I did not want to appear like a hick from a small town, so I (again) didn't ask any questions about the menu and simply pointed to a menu selection. As I recall, I had chosen something called *Kaninchen eintopf*, or some other German name that meant nothing to me. The waiter stood there and stared at me. I didn't know if I was supposed to tip him or what, so I asked him if there was something wrong. He replied by asking me if I knew what I was ordering. When I hesitated, he explained that I was ordering rabbit stew. I changed my order to prime rib.

Ordering Side Dishes

Use these phrases when ordering side dishes:

to audio file 08e Ordering a side dish.

Please bring me a side order of:	*Por favor tráigame un plato adicional de:*
I would like to order:	*Me gustaría ordenar:*
peas.	*los chícharos.*
a baked potato.	*una papa asada al horno.*
a baked potato with chives.	*una papa asada al horno con cebollinos.*
boiled potatoes.	*las papas hervidas.*
fried potatoes.	*las papas fritas.*
French fries.	*las papas fritas a la francesa.*
carrots.	*las zanahorias.*
cheese.	*el queso.*
cucumber in the salad.	*el pepino en la ensalada.*
fruit.	*la fruta.*
mixed vegetables.	*los vegetales mixtos.*
sweet potato.	*el camote.*
a salad.	*una ensalada.*
Sautéed onions.	*las cebollas sofritas.*
some bread.	*el pan.*

Ordering Beverages

You can use these phrases to order beverages:

Go to audio file 08f Ordering a beverage and dessert.

I would like to order:	*Me gustaría ordenar:*
apple juice.	*el jugo de manzana.*

a pot of coffee.	*una cazuela de café.*
a cup of coffee.	*una taza de café.*
a cup of coffee, black.	*una taza de café, negro.*
a cup of coffee with sugar and cream.	*una taza de café con azúcar y crema.*
a cup of coffee with low-calorie sugar.	*una taza de café con azúcar bajo en calorías.*
a cup of coffee with sugar.	*una taza de café con azúcar.*
a glass of milk.	*un vaso de leche.*
a glass of orange juice.	*un vaso de jugo de naranja.*
a glass of water.	*un vaso de agua.*
some herbal tea.	*un té de hierbas.*
a cup of hot tea.	*una taza de té caliente.*
a glass of iced tea.	*un vaso de té helado.*
lemon juice.	*el jugo de limón.*
a lemonade.	*una limonada.*

Ordering Desserts

And finally, you can use these phrases to order dessert:

a slice of cake.	*Una rebanada de queque.*
a slice of pie.	*Una rebanada de pastel.*
a dish of chocolate ice cream.	*Un plato de helado de chocolate.*
a dish of mixed fruit.	*Un plato de fruta mixta.*

Learning to Pronounce the Names of Popular Dishes

Go to audio file 08g Mexican menu names.

At this point we will provide you the proper pronunciation for a few Mexican menu items. The main purpose is to teach you how to pronounce these names when you see them in a Mexican menu. The name of the dishes will be pronounced for you in an audio file; there is no English pronunciation in the audio for these names.

Here are some popular dishes you might order in a Mexican restaurant:

- *El guacamole*: An appetizer made with avocado, cilantro, a chile salsa, finely diced onion, diced tomato, and a dash of lime juice. It can be eaten as a dip with tostadas (fried corn tortilla chips).

- *Los chiles rellenos*: Green chile peppers stuffed with cheddar, Monterrey jack, or mozzarella cheese, dipped in an egg batter and fried in vegetable oil. Served with beans and rice.

- *Las enchiladas*: Deep-fried corn tortillas smothered with green or red chile, cheese, and onions. Served either in a stack (flat), with fried beans and rice, or rolled in a casserole.

- *Las sopaipillas*: Deep-fried slices of dough, cut into triangles, squares, or any other shape. They come out puffed, with an air pocket in the middle that you can stuff with anything you can think of. Popular stuffings are refried beans, green or red chile, cheese, and a little bit of lettuce and tomato. A mouth-watering favorite is to sprinkle the sopaipilla with powdered or regular sugar, or eat it plain with a little bit of honey poured over it.

WHY MEXICANS SING

Many people erroneously think that Mexicans sing because of what they drink. That is not true. They sing because of what they eat!

If you get the chance, you should try Mexican dishes you read about in this section of the chapter. Order some of the hot chile and you will be singing too.

The following are just a few additional menu items that you will find at Mexican restaurants. Generally, menus provide a brief description of each menu entry in English and Spanish, but we describe them here, as well:

- *El plato de la combinación*: Typically, this plate contains a combination of three main food items (such as a rolled *enchilada*, a *taco*, a *tamale*, or a *chile relleno*) plus rice, beans, green or red chile with meat, and lettuce and tomato. Tamales are explained in the "What Is Nixtamal?" talking point later in this chapter.

- *Los burritos:* The *burrito* has become a favorite fast food item. It is made with a *tortilla* that is stuffed with your favorite food and then rolled. Popular stuffings are hamburger meat, beans, meat and potatoes, bacon and eggs, and chili with meat.

- *El menudo:* This is a stew made with hominy, red chile, and meat.

- *Los tacos:* These are corn tortillas stuffed with hamburger meat, lettuce, and tomatoes. Tacos can also be made with shredded chicken meat, or beans.

Understanding the Ingredients in Hispanic Dishes

Go to audio file 08h The ingredients.

In this section, you learn the names of ingredients used in cooking Hispanic foods. Some of the spices and other ingredients are what give Hispanic food that unique taste (Chapter 7, "Shopping," lists the names of other food items). Most of these items also are used in the preparation of American cuisine:

baking powder	el polvo de hornear
barbeque steak sauce	la salsa de barbacoa para el bistec
butter	la mantequilla
cabbage	el repollo
chickpea	el garbanzo
coconut	el coco
coriander	el cilantro
corn dough	la masa de harina de maíz
flour	la harina
garlic	el ajo
green beans	las habichuelas verdes
ground hominy	el nixtamal
lard	la manteca de cerdo
lettuce	la lechuga
margarine	la margarina
melted cheese dip	el chile con queso
syrup	el jarabe
tabasco sauce	la salsa tabasco
vermicelli	el fideo
white mexican cheese	el asadero

WHAT IS NIXTAMAL?

The *nixtamal* is dough made from ground hominy, the corn used to make grits. As its name suggests, this dough is used to make corn tortillas and *tamales*. To make *tamales*, the dough is stuffed with meat and red or green chile. It is then wrapped in cornhusks and cooked. To eat them, you remove the cornhusk and eat them with a fork or by hand. The taste is just as delicious either way.

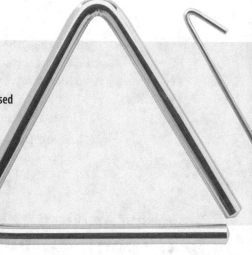

Paying for Your Meal

Go to audio file 08i Paying and complaints.

Payment options vary in different restaurants. At some restaurants you can pay by personal check, credit card, debit card, or cash. Others restrict how you may pay. Some restaurants require that you pay your server; others require that you go to a cashier. In this section, you learn the terms and phrases you can use to handle most of these situations.

To request a bill or a check you say:

Please let me have my bill.	Por favor deme mi cuenta.
Please bring me the check.	Por favor tráigame el cheque.
Please include all of us in one bill.	Por favor incluya a todos en una cuenta.
Please give us separate checks.	Por favor denos cheques separados.

To inquire about required forms of payment, and where to pay you can use the following:

Do you accept credit cards?	¿Acepta usted tarjetas de crédito?
Do you accept personal checks?	¿Acepta usted cheques personales?
Do you accept debit cards?	¿Acepta usted tarjetas de débito?
Do you accept traveler's checks?	¿Acepta usted cheques de viajero?
May I include the tip in the payment to the cashier?	¿Puedo incluir la propina en el pago al cajero?
Do I pay you or the cashier?	¿Le pago a usted o al cajero?
You can pay me.	Usted me puede pagar.
You have to pay the cashier.	Usted tiene que pagar al cajero.
You can pay either way.	Usted puede pagar de una u otra manera.

Registering Complaints

Unfortunately there are times when we have to bring something to management's attention, even at the best restaurants.

To call a waiter's or waitress' attention you have to call him or her as follows:

Sir!	¡Señor!
Young man!	¡Joven!
Ma'am!	¡Señora!
(If you are sure the lady is married)	
Miss!	¡Señorita!
(If you are sure she is not married, or just don't know.)	
Please call the manager.	Por favor llame al gerente.
I wish to speak with the manager.	Deseo hablar con el gerente.
Let me talk with whoever is in charge.	Déjeme hablar con cualquier persona que esté encargada.
May I speak with you, please?	¿Puedo hablar con usted, por favor?
My food is cold.	Mi comida está fría.
This is not what I ordered.	Esto no es lo que yo ordené.
The steak was not cooked to order.	El bistec no se cocinó como lo ordené.
I was not provided silverware.	No se me proveyó la vajilla de plata.
The tableware is dirty.	El servicio de mesa está sucio.
My table is dirty.	Mi mesa está sucia.
The chairs are not clean.	Las sillas no están limpias.
I was charged an erroneous amount.	Se me cobró una cantidad errónea.
My bill is not correct.	Mi cuenta no está correcta.
I asked for and was not brought a high chair for my child.	Pedí y no se me trajo una silla alta para mi niño.

Asking for Assistance

Sometimes you need to ask for assistance in any restaurant. You may be asking for directions to the restroom, or need a place to change your baby's diaper. Other times, your needs may be more dramatic, as when you become ill or someone you're dining with suffers from a choking accident. Any such incident is made worse when you do not speak the language and therefore cannot ask for assistance. The text in this section helps you quickly learn some key phrases and sentences for requesting assistance when dining in a restaurant where the majority of the staff and customers speak Spanish.

Finding the Powder Room

Here are some questions and responses that will help you as you ask for directions to the restroom:

Go to audio file 08j The powder room

Where is the powder room?	¿Dónde está el tocador de señoras?
Where is the bathroom?	¿Dónde está el cuarto de baño?

Possible responses are:

The bathroom is over there. (The employee may simply point to it.)	El cuarto de baño está allá.
The bathroom is to the right of the kitchen.	El cuarto de baño está a la derecha de la cocina.
The bathroom is to the left of the kitchen.	El cuarto de baño está a la izquierda de la cocina.
It does not have a table for changing diapers.	No tiene una mesa para cambiar pañales.
It does have a table for changing diapers.	Sí tiene una mesa para cambiar pañales.

Asking for Medical Assistance

The ability to obtain quick medical assistance for yourself or someone in your party in a life-threatening situation may save someone's life. This section includes material that may prepare you for a situation that you hope will never happen. These phrases and sentences will help you if you need to request medical assistance in a Hispanic restaurant:

Go to audio file 08k Medical assistance.

Please call 911!	¡Por favor llame a 911!
Here is my cell phone.	Aquí está mi teléfono celular.
Please call an ambulance.	Por favor llame una ambulancia.
Please call the police.	Por favor llame a la policía.
Ask if there is a doctor in the restaurant.	Pregunte si hay un médico en el restaurante.
Is there a telephone I can use?	¿Hay un teléfono que puedo usar?

I am feeling ill.	*Me siento enfermo/a.*
Help! My friend is choking!	*¡Auxilio! ¡Mi amigo se atraganta!*

Summary

The material in this chapter taught you how to find a restaurant that serves authentic Hispanic food. You also learned how to determine whether reservations were required, and how to make them. You also learned some phrases and sentences you'll use when ordering from the menu or inquiring about the ingredients in dishes. You learned how to request and settle the bill and how to report problems to the proper staff member in the restaurant. You were also provided a glimpse of some of the ingredients that play a role in giving some Hispanic dishes that unique taste. Finally, you are now prepared in the event that there is some incident that requires an emergency trip to the powder room or to a medical facility.

In the next chapter you will be provided more detailed information on how to manage your health. You will learn to discuss wellness issues. You will be provided an extensive amount of detail on how to discuss your condition with the medical staff, and how to fulfill the requirements for being admitted to a medical facility. The chapter includes a section that can prove very useful if you should need to purchase medication at a Hispanic pharmacy. We will teach you how to participate in casual conversation on two topics that are probably the most discussed topics around—diet and exercise.

Audio Files

- [ ] 09a Social conversation about health
- [ ] 09b Physical exams and test results
- [ ] 09c Healthy practices and remedies
- [ ] 09d Going to the doctor
- [ ] 09e Scheduling an appointment
- [ ] 09f Talking with your doctor
- [ ] 09g Questions for your doctor
- [ ] 09h Providing insurance information
- [ ] 09i Being admitted to the hospital
- [ ] 09j Using the pharmacy
- [ ] 09k Talking about diet and weight loss
- [ ] 09l Describing exercises and equipment

9

In this chapter:

- ❋ Talking about good health, illnesses, and good health practices
- ❋ Getting medical help from a doctor or hospital
- ❋ Talking about diet, exercise, and weight loss

Managing Your Health

Health news is part of almost every television newscast. Health, diet, and exercise are discussed in daily talk shows. Consequently, they have all of us talking about health-related issues.

The Spanish terms, phrases, and sentences you learn in this chapter will help you involve yourself in social conversation about what you and your Spanish-speaking companions are doing to stay well, what illnesses you might have, and what you are doing to overcome them. If you are in a situation where you have to go to a Hispanic doctor, you can use the information you learn here to make an appointment and describe your symptoms to the physician from an extensive list of possible illnesses and diseases. You also learn how to discuss insurance and the claims process in Spanish. In the event that you are admitted to a hospital, you can take advantage of the Spanish words you learn here to handle the admissions process.

The high cost of prescription drugs in the U.S. has driven many to buy medication out of country. The price differences are incredible, and if you read the information included with the medication, it is identical to what is sold in U.S. pharmacies. Even if you are not in the market to pursue that avenue, you may find yourself in a situation where you have to fill a prescription at a Hispanic pharmacy. We will provide you the translated material, with audio, to be able to do that.

We will wrap up this chapter with social talk you can have about diet, exercise, and what exercise equipment is the most effective for losing weight.

Social Conversation About Health

Go to audio file 09a Social conversation about health.

There are many health-related issues that can be discussed in a social conversation. Let us start out with a general conversation about health. In this example, two friends are talking about their health.

How is your health?	*¿Cómo está tu salud?*
I'm feeling fine—how about you?	*Me siento bien—¿y tú?*
I am doing okay, for my age.	*Me va bien, para mi edad.*
I have a lot of stress.	*Tengo mucha tensión nerviosa.*
My eyesight is not that good.	*Mi vista no está muy bien.*
I have lost a lot of my hearing.	*He perdido mucho de mi oído.*
Have you told your doctor about your problems?	*¿Le has contado a tu médico sobre tus problemas?*
I have not been to a doctor in 10 years.	*No he ido a un médico en diez años.*
You need a physical examination.	*Necesitas un examen físico.*

Talking About Physical Exams and Medical Test Results

It is a wonderful feeling when we go through a battery of tests as part of a physical examination, and the doctor tells us that the results indicate that everything is fine. We come out of the doctor's office, dash home or back to work, and start talking about the examination results. We want everyone to know that we are in good health. And sometimes, everyone wants to know what we are doing to stay in such good health. There are also those cases when the test results indicate that there is a medical problem that needs to be addressed. Here are some expressions that might be used in conversations about visits to the doctor, physical exams, and medical test results.

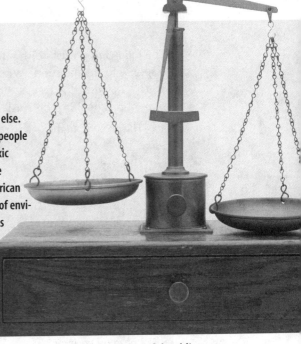

HEALTH ISSUES IN LATIN AMERICA

Like everyone, Hispanics value good health above all else. Unfortunately, one of the biggest health issues that people from Latin American countries face is exposure to toxic waste. Large industrial companies from the U.S. have moved their manufacturing operations to Latin American countries to take advantage of cheap labor and lack of environmental controls. The result is that Latin Americans are exposed to toxic waste and high levels of mercury contamination, which often gets into their drinking water. For these Hispanics, industries moving into their communities bring more jobs, but at a high cost to their health.

I just got out of the doctor's office.   *Acabo de salir de la oficina del médico.*

The preceding statement may prompt the following question:

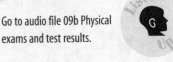

Go to audio file 09b Physical exams and test results.

What did the doctor tell you?	¿Qué le dijo el médico?
The doctor told me:	El médico me dijo:
Everything is fine.	Todo está bien.
All the test results came back negative.	Todos los resultados experimentales fueron negativos.
My sugar levels are normal.	Mis niveles de azúcar están normales.
My blood pressure was 125 over 82.	Mi presión sanguínea fue ciento veinticinco sobre ochenta y dos.
I have no heart damage.	No tengo daño del corazón.
The X-rays were negative.	Los rayos x (equis) fueron negativos.

I do not have cancer.	No tengo cáncer.
I am pregnant.	Estoy embarazada.
I am going to have twins.	Voy a tener unos gemelos.
That is good news.	Ésas son buenas noticias.

The following phrases also might be given in response to the question "What did the doctor tell you?" They describe results that indicate the patient has health problems:

The doctor told me:	El médico me dijo:
I am sick.	Estoy enfermo.
I have high blood pressure.	Tengo presión alta de sangre.
My good cholesterol is low.	Mi colesterol bueno está bajo.
My bad cholesterol is high.	Mi colesterol malo está elevado.
I need a pacemaker.	Necesito un marcapasos.
I have arthritis in my hip.	Tengo artritis en la cadera.
I have diabetes.	Tengo diabetes.
I need glasses.	Necesito anteojos.
I need a hearing aid.	Necesito un audífono.
I need to lose weight.	Necesito perder peso.
I have carpal tunnel syndrome.	Tengo síndrome carpiano del túnel.

To any of this bad medical news, you might respond with comments similar to these:

Really?	¿De veras?
No way!	¡No me digas!
How difficult for you.	Qué difícil para ti.
I'm sorry to hear that.	Siento mucho oír eso.
I hope you get better.	Espero que te mejores.
What can I do to help?	¿En qué puedo ayudarte?
Will you be in the hospital?	¿Estarás en el hospital?
I'm praying for you.	Estoy orando para ti.

> **note** Joking about medical maladies and experiences isn't limited to any one culture. After you've been to the doctor, your Spanish-speaking friends or co-workers might joke with you about the experience. Here are some humorous questions they might ask about your visit:
>
> | Well, are you going to live? | ¿Pues bien, vas a vivir? |
> | Did you suffer cardiac arrest when you got the bill? | ¿Sufriste tú paro cardíaco cuando tú obtuviste la cuenta? |

Discussing Healthy Practices and Remedies

Casual conversations about health don't always focus on sickness and bad news. Sometimes people like to compare notes on how they maintain *good* health. The example sentences in this section might be heard in any conversation between friends about achieving and maintaining good health:

Go to audio file 09c Healthy practices and remedies.

What are you doing to stay healthy?	¿Qué haces tú para permanecer saludable?
What did you do to lower your sugar levels?	¿Qué hiciste tú para aminorar tus niveles de azúcar?
I have a good doctor.	Tengo un buen médico.
I guess I just have good genes.	Creo que tengo buenos genes.
My grandparents lived to be 100 years old.	Mis abuelos vivieron hasta tener cien años de edad.
I'm drinking eight glasses of water a day.	Bebo ocho vasos de agua al día.
I am taking vitamins.	Tomo vitaminas.
I quit eating doughnuts at the office.	Dejé de comer donas en la oficina.
I became a vegetarian.	Me convertí en un vegetariano.
I gave up caffeine.	Dejé la cafeína.
I cut back on the coffee.	Recorté el café.
I only have one soft drink a day.	Sólo tengo un refresco al día.

HEALTHY HISPANIC DIET

When most people think about Hispanic food, they think of Mexican food like that described in Chapter 8, "Eating Out." Most of that food is delicious, but probably not the best for our health. That food is not representative of food consumed by people in other Latin American countries. Most Hispanic diets are very healthy. The Hispanic diet includes a large variety fish, shellfish, poultry, vegetables, beans, whole grains, nuts, and fresh fruits. These are things that everyone should eat as part of their regular diet.

Going to the Doctor or Hospital

Go to audio file 09d Going to the doctor.

Whether you're seeing your regular doctor or a specialist, you must be able to describe your injury, illness, or symptoms. In this section of the chapter, we provide a few examples of conversations that might take place as you or someone else decides that there is a need to go to the doctor. You learn how to schedule an appointment, describe your symptoms, and handle the dreaded insurance questions. This section also describes some of the expressions you'll use if you or someone you know must be admitted to the hospital, as well as sentences you'll find useful when filling prescriptions at the pharmacy.

Explaining That You Need to See a Doctor

To tell someone in Spanish that you need to see a doctor, you might use these sentences:

I need a doctor because:	*Necesito a un médico porque:*
I have a pain in my stomach.	*Tengo un dolor en el estómago.*
I have chest pain.	*Tengo dolor en el pecho.*
I am having contractions.	*Estoy teniendo contracciones.*
I am so sick that I need immediate attention.	*Estoy tan enfermo que necesito atención inmediata.*

Here are some potential responses to the preceding statements:

Did you call your doctor?	*¿Llamaste a tu médico?*
Do you want me to call a doctor?	*¿Quieres que llame a un médico?*
I left a message with your doctor's answering service.	*Dejé un mensaje con el servicio de contestación de tu médico.*
You will be referred to a doctor that is on call.	*Tú serás referido a un médico que está de guardia médica.*
Your regular doctor will refer you to a specialist.	*Tu médico regular te referirá a un en especialista.*
You can get immediate attention in the hospital emergency room.	*Tú puedes obtener atención inmediata en el cuarto de emergencia del hospital.*

The following are examples of statements you might make if you require the services of a dentist or ophthalmologist.

I need to see a dentist.	*Necesito ver a un dentista.*
I broke a tooth.	*Rompí un diente.*
I'm in a lot of pain.	*Estoy en mucho dolor.*
I've lost a filling.	*He perdido una calza de los dientes.*
One of my molars has a cavity.	*Una de mis muelas tiene una cavidad.*
I lost my glasses.	*Perdí mis anteojos.*
I broke one of the lenses.	*Rompí uno de los lentes.*
I injured my left eye.	*Dañé el ojo izquierdo.*
I need to renew the prescription for my contact lenses.	*Necesito renovar la receta para mis lentes de contacto.*

Scheduling an Appointment

An appointment to see the doctor is normally scheduled over the telephone, or at the time that one is finishing up at the doctor's office. There is nothing really complicated about this process, but communicating in a foreign language can make things a bit more difficult. In this section, we give you some sample sentences to help reduce that difficulty.

If you call a Hispanic doctor's office during normal office hours, a person should answer your call. If you call when the office is closed, you will probably get a response from an answering service. Your call to schedule an appointment will include some of the following sentences. In this example, the Hispanic receptionist is answering your call:

Hello.	*¿Bueno?*
Hello.	*Dígame.*

If you or the receptionist don't understand the initial greeting, you might use these sentences:

Pardon me?	*¿Mande?*
Please repeat what you said.	*Por favor repita lo que usted dijo.*

> **Speaking of...**
> In making a doctor's appointment, you will need to use the dates and time information you learned in the "Dates" and "Times" sections of Chapter 2, "Letters, Numbers, Dates, and Dollars." You may want to refresh your memory by listening to the audio on the specific numbers you will need to make the appointment.

> **Listen Up**
>
> Go to audio file 09e
> Scheduling an appointment.

> **tip**
> If the person answers the telephone with a "Hello," that normally means that he or she speaks English. If they answer in Spanish, they may not speak English.

You can then proceed to make the appointment. Here is a sample conversation on this topic:

May I help you?	*¿Le puedo asistir?*
I wish to see the doctor.	*Deseo ver al médico.*
I must see the doctor right away.	*Necesito ver al médico de inmediato.*
Do you have an appointment?	*¿Tiene una cita?*
Yes, I do.	*Sí, tengo una cita.*
No, I don't.	*No, no tengo una cita.*
I wish to make an appointment.	*Deseo hacer una cita.*
Do you have any preference on the date and time?	*¿Tiene usted cualquiera preferencia en la fecha y el tiempo?*
I have no preference.	*No tengo preferencia.*
I can be there anytime.	*Puedo estar allí cuando sea.*
I cannot go in before noon.	*No puedo ir antes del mediodía.*
Can you come in this afternoon at 3:00 p.m.?	*¿Puede venir usted esta tarde a las tres de la tarde?*
Your appointment is for Wednesday, next week at 2:30 p.m.	*Su cita es para el miércoles, la semana próxima a las dos y media de la tarde.*
The doctor is out of town.	*El médico está de viaje.*
I am about to give birth to my baby.	*Estoy a punto de dar a luz a mi bebé.*
Please go to the emergency room at the hospital.	*Por favor vaya al cuarto de emergencia en el hospital.*

ANSWERING THE TELEPHONE

When a Hispanic person answers the telephone, they say *Bueno?* ("Well?"), or *Dígame* ("Tell me") instead of the Spanish equivalent for "Hello." If the Hispanic person wishes for you to repeat something, she will say *Mande?*, which means "Pardon me," or she might ask you to repeat whatever you said. You will be provided the audio for these Spanish words within this section.

Talking with Your Doctor

If you are able to describe your symptoms in some detail, the chances are your doctor will be better able to prescribe medication or a procedure that will solve your medical problem. This section

Go to audio file 09f Talking with your doctor.

provides a significant amount of detail that may be useful if you ever are attended by a Hispanic medical doctor.

Let's begin with questions and statements the doctor and her staff might ask or say to a patient:

How can I help you?	*¿Cómo le puedo ayudar?*
Step on the scale.	*Súbase a la pesa.*
I need a urine sample.	*Necesito una prueba de la orina.*
I'm going to take your blood pressure.	*Voy a tomar su tensión arterial.*
I'm going to take your temperature.	*Voy a tomar su temperatura.*
I'm going to look in your ears, nose, and mouth.	*Voy a mirar en las orejas, la nariz, y la boca.*
I'm going to listen to your breathing.	*Voy a escuchar su respiración.*
Cough.	*Tosa.*
I'm going to feel your stomach.	*Voy a palpar el estómago.*
I'm going to listen to your heart.	*Voy a escuchar el corazón.*
I'm going to check the reflexes in your knee.	*Voy a examinar los reflejos en la rodilla.*
What medication are you taking?	*¿Qué medicamentos está tomando?*
What other symptoms do you have?	*¿Qué otros síntomas tiene?*
Where does it hurt?	*¿Dónde le duele?*

The following phrases describe a simple way to talk about where it hurts in a singular body part using the phrase *Me duele*.

I have pain:	*Me duele:*
in my back.	*la espalda.*
in my shoulder.	*el hombro.*
in my throat.	*la garganta.*
in my stomach.	*el estómago.*
in my breast.	*el seno.*
in my chest.	*el pecho.*
in my kneecap.	*la rótula.*
in my hip when I walk.	*la cadera cuando camino.*
in my neck.	*el cuello.*

The following examples show you how to say that you have pain in plural body parts by using the introductory phrase *Me duelen.*

I have pain:	Me duelen:
in my ears.	los oídos.
in my kidneys.	los riñones.
in my knuckles.	los nudillos.
in my feet.	los pies.
in my knees.	las rodillas

Other possible responses that the patient might give to the doctor are as follows:

I am in the eighth month of pregnancy.	Estoy en el octavo mes de embarazo.
I can't sleep.	No puedo dormir.
I have nausea.	Tengo náusea.
I feel weak.	Me siento débil.
I have a cold.	Estoy resfriado.
I have a migraine headache.	Tengo un dolor de cabeza de migraña.
I have the flu.	Tengo la gripe.

You also might want to ask the doctor some questions, as shown in the examples that follow. Most of the responses to these questions require only a yes or no answer, so those answers are excluded:

> Go to audio file 09g Questions for your doctor.

Is my condition serious?	¿Es mi condición grave?
Is my disease contagious?	¿Es mi enfermedad contagiosa?
How long should I stay in bed?	¿Cuánto tiempo debería quedarme en cama?
You should stay in bed for one week.	Usted debería quedarse en cama por una semana.
How frequently should I take the medication?	¿Con qué frecuencia debería tomar la medicación?
Follow the instructions on the medicine bottle.	Siga las instrucciones en la botella de la medicina.
Do I need to see you again?	¿Necesito verle otra vez?
Can you prescribe generic medication?	¿Puede prescribir usted medicación genérica?

Providing insurance information

Generally doctor's offices require insurance information only when you go to them for the first time or when there has been a change in health insurance policy. They make a copy of the insurance card, and retain it for future visits. They also have the various insurance forms, and will file them for the patient. At a doctor's office in the United States, there is very little dialogue during the checkout process if you have previously provided them your insurance information.

PAYING FOR MEDICAL SERVICES IN LATIN AMERICAN COUNTRIES

Doctors and hospitals in Mexico and Central or South America will not accept U.S. health insurance policies. If you were to require hospitalization in Argentina, for example, you would have to produce either an international travel medical insurance policy or pay cash for your treatment. You would then have to file a claim with your stateside health insurance provider. You may discover that your health insurance provider offers limited coverage when you are traveling in other countries. U.S. citizens are advised to take out full international medical insurance when visiting Latin American countries.

The following sentences provide a sampling of the conversation that may transpire upon checking in at the doctor's office:

Go to audio file 09h Providing insurance information.

Do you have health insurance?	¿Tiene usted seguro de salud?
May I see your insurance card?	¿Puedo ver su tarjeta de seguro?
Here is my insurance card.	Aquí está mi tarjeta de seguro.
Is your address shown here current?	¿Está su dirección mostrada aquí corriente?
What is your social security number?	¿Cuál es su número de seguro social?
What is your date of birth?	¿Cuál es su fecha de nacimiento?
I will make a copy of your insurance card for our records.	Copiaré su tarjeta de seguro para nuestros registros.

You are required to pay the copay amount up front.	Usted está obligado a pagar la cantidad del pago colateral por delante.
What company is your primary insurer?	¿Qué compañía es su asegurador primario?
Are you under Medicare?	¿Está usted bajo el seguro medico del Estado?
Here is my Medicare card.	Aquí está mi tarjeta del seguro medico del Estado.
Your bill for today's services is $398.45.	Su cuenta por los servicios de hoy es trescientos noventa y ocho dólares y cuarenta y cinco centavos.
How do you plan to pay for this amount?	¿Cómo intenta usted pagar esta cantidad?
Will you please file the claim for me?	Puede usted enviar el reporte de la reclamación para mí, por favor?
The doctor's office cannot file those claims for you.	La oficina del médico no puede reportar esas reclamaciones para usted.
You have to pay the full amount today.	Usted tiene que pagar la cantidad total hoy.
I will pay in cash.	Pagaré en efectivo.
Do you accept personal checks?	¿Acepta usted cheques personales?

Being Admitted to the Hospital

The health insurance questions and statements listed in the previous section will also be useful if you are admitted to a hospital. The admissions clerk might ask you a number of questions and enter the answers directly into a computer. That beats having to fill out the form manually! This section lists some of those questions.

Go to audio file 09i Being admitted to the hospital.

What is your full name?	¿Cuál es su nombre y apellidos?
What is your address?	¿Cuál es su dirección?
What is your social security number?	¿Cuál es su número de seguro social?
May I see your driver's license?	¿Puedo ver su licencia de conducir?
Are you married?	¿Está usted casado?

How many dependents do you have?	¿Cuántos dependientes tiene usted?
Who do we notify in case of emergency?	¿A quién notificamos en caso de la emergencia?
When is the last time you were in a hospital?	¿Cuándo es la última vez que usted estuvo en un hospital?
Have you had any major surgeries within the past five years?	¿Ha tenido usted cualquier cirugías mayores dentro de los últimos cinco años?
Do you smoke?	¿Fuma usted?
Are you allergic to any medications?	¿Está usted alérgico a unos medicamentos?
I am allergic to penicillin and sulfa.	Soy alérgico a la penicilina y sulfa.
Please put all your personal belongings in this bag.	Por favor ponga todos sus efectos personales en esta bolsa.
Do you have any questions?	¿Tiene usted cualquiera pregunta?
Please follow the nurse to your room.	Por favor siga a la enfermera a su cuarto.

HISPANIC SURNAMES

In the Hispanic world, most people use two surnames or *apellidos*. The first name used is their father's first surname, and the second their mother's first surname. The surnames for the children of Samuel *Soto* Ruiz and Juana *Vega* Lozano would be *Soto Vega*.

Using the Pharmacy

It is highly advisable that you have a prescription issued by a medical doctor before attempting to purchase prescription drugs at a pharmacy. That's the best way to ensure that the strengths and dosages are accurate. The following translations will help you fill a prescription and purchase over-the-counter medication at a Hispanic pharmacy.

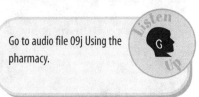

Go to audio file 09j Using the pharmacy.

BUYING PRESCRIPTION DRUGS IN LATIN AMERICAN COUNTRIES

Though prescriptions are required by U.S. pharmacies, in some Latin American countries, some pharmacies will sell prescription drugs without a prescription. The same pharmaceutical companies that sell their products through U.S. pharmacies manufacture the medications sold in Latin American pharmacies. And identical drugs can have different prices in the U.S. and foreign markets.

Where can I find a pharmacy?	¿Dónde puedo encontrar una farmacia?
What time does the pharmacy open?	¿A qué hora se abre la farmacia?
I would like to have this prescription filled.	Me gustaría llenar esta receta.
I need over-the-counter medication for:	Necesito medicación disponible sin receta para:
a chest cold.	un catarro bronquial.
a migraine headache.	un dolor de cabeza de migraña.
allergies.	las alergias.
an upset stomach.	un malestar estomacal.
motion sickness.	el mareo por movimiento.
I am searching for:	Busco:
a thermometer.	un termómetro.
Band-Aids.	las Curitas.
cough drops.	las pastillas para la tos.
gauze.	la gasa.
nose spray.	la rociada nasal.
the aspirins.	las aspirinas.
vitamins.	las vitaminas.

Discussions About Diet and Exercise

The slender bodies and flat bellies portrayed in advertising on television and magazines make all of us feel the need to shed a few pounds. Unfortunately there is no easy way to lose weight and tighten those muscles that have gone soft. Diet is a sacrifice and exercise is hard work. So what are we going to do? I guess we can at least talk about them! In this section we will talk about what we are doing to cut back on our carbohydrates and calorie intake. If we happen to overindulge, we will talk about what exercises and equipment are out there to help us get back on track.

Go to audio file 09k Talking about diet and weight loss.

Talking About Diet and Weight Loss

As much as we profess that we hate the subject of dieting, we always wind up talking about it. If you don't bring it up, someone else will. In this section, you learn some sample sentences for talking about eating habits, fad diets, and weight loss.

These sentences are in conversational form:

You look great.	*Usted se ve estupenda.*
Have you lost weight?	*¿Ha perdido usted peso?*
How many pounds have you lost?	*¿Cuántas libras ha perdido usted?*
I lost fifteen pounds in one month.	*Perdí quince libras en un mes.*
What did you do to lose weight?	*¿Qué hizo usted para perder peso?*
I went on a diet.	*Me puse a dieta.*
What regimen did you follow?	*¿Qué régimen siguió usted?*
I quit eating bread.	*Dejé de comer pan.*
I gave up the tortillas.	*Dejé las tortillas.*
I do not eat any sweets.	*No como ningunos dulces.*
I became a vegetarian.	*Me convertí en vegetariano.*
I have been a vegetarian for years.	*He sido vegetariana por años.*
I cut back on my calorie intake.	*Recorté mi toma de calorías.*
I am not on a diet.	*No estoy a dieta.*
I went on a low-carbohydrate intake.	*Me puse en un régimen de carbohidratos bajos.*
I am using some diet pills.	*Estoy usando unas píldoras de dieta.*
I am using a diet patch.	*Estoy usando un parche de dieta.*

Describing Exercises and Exercise Equipment

If you belong to a health club or gym, you do not have to worry about making an investment in exercise equipment. If you decide to purchase your own equipment for whatever reasons, be

Go to audio file 09l Describing exercises and equipment

prepared to go through a serious workout. There is so much exercise equipment being marketed that it is difficult to decide what to buy. You can use the following sentences to talk about what you are doing to stay in shape:

You look terrific!	*¡Usted se ve terrífico!*
What are you doing to stay in shape?	*¿Qué estás haciendo para permanecer en forma?*
Do you belong to a health club or gymnasium?	*¿Perteneces a un club de salud o gimnasio?*
Do you have your own exercise equipment?	*¿Tienes equipo de ejercicio?*

Here are some statements you might make in response to the preceding questions or to describe your solution for staying in shape:

I lost 30 pounds through exercise.	*Perdí treinta libras a través del ejercicio.*
I walk on the treadmill for 30 minutes, five days a week.	*Camino sobre la rueda de molino por treinta minutos, cinco días de la semana.*
I run two miles on the treadmill every day.	*Corro dos millas en la rueda de molino todos los días.*
I do abdominal exercises.	*Hago ejercicios abdominales.*
I started lifting weights.	*Inicié el levantamiento de pesas.*
My company established a workout room with lots of exercise equipment.	*Mi compañía estableció un cuarto de entrenamiento con montones de equipo de ejercicio.*
I joined a health club that is open 24 hours a day.	*Me uní a un club de salud que está abierto veinticuatro horas al día.*
I bought:	*Compré:*
a stair climb machine.	*Una máquina de subida de la escalera.*
an exercise bicycle.	*Una bicicleta de ejercicio.*
an elliptical training machine.	*Una máquina elíptica de entrenamiento.*
I work out for forty-five minutes on the stair climb machine.	*Me ejercito por cuarenta y cinco minutos en la máquina de subida de la escalera.*
I ride the exercise bicycle for thirty minutes every other day.	*Monto la bicicleta de ejercicio por treinta minutos cada día de por medio.*
I use the elliptical training machine for one hour three times a week.	*Uso la máquina elíptica de entrenamiento por una hora tres veces por semana.*

Summary

In this chapter you learned how to talk about the health issues that are on the minds of most people today. You were provided with an extensive amount of translated material that will allow you to participate in talk about being well, being sick, and fitness and health practices you might follow. You learned how to schedule an appointment with the doctor, or check in to a hospital, should that become necessary. You also learned how to describe your symptoms to a Hispanic doctor, or to some other person in casual conversation. This chapter also listed a number of sentences and expressions you'll find useful if you ever want to purchase medication at a Hispanic pharmacy. You also learned how to talk about the diet, exercises, and workout equipment you are using to manage your weight.

In the next chapter you will be provided material that can be very useful if you need any kind of services at a hotel staffed by Hispanic employees who do not understand English. If you are able to communicate with the staff in their own language, they will be better able to respond to your needs. You will be able to get assistance checking in and make your stay at the hotel more comfortable.

Part III

Special Situations

Audio Files

10

In this chapter:

- ✳ Making reservations
- ✳ Checking into the hotel and getting assistance and information on the amenities and services
- ✳ Arranging for ground transportation
- ✳ Traveling between the airport and the hotel
- ✳ Ensuring that the room is in good order
- ✳ Using the telephone

Staying at a Hotel

Staying at a hotel can be wonderful experience; it can also be a nightmare. When we are on a business trip, we can settle for a warm bath, a comfortable bed, good reception on the TV, and good food at the restaurant. When we are on vacation and plan to stay a few days at the hotel, we expect a little more. The hotel has to be more than a home away from home. We should be able to relax and enjoy ourselves. A good hotel is prepared to provide for our every need. We must, however, communicate any deficiencies to the hotel staff in order to get them resolved.

The material in this chapter and other parts of this book will allow you to expand your choices of vacation destinations for you and your family. You can now take your family to a tropical paradise in some Latin American country, and stay at a five-star hotel by the beach for a lot less money than what it would cost you for a similar vacation in the U.S. There is no greater feeling than to be sitting in the balcony of your suite, by the beach, with the cool ocean breeze blowing in your face. We're not in the travel business, but just for the fun of it enter "vacation in Latin America" or "vacation in Mexico" in your search engine and look at the options you get. *Hasta la vista!* (See you later!)

Many hotels in the U.S. hire maintenance employees from other countries that cannot speak English. Your contact with such a hotel may be through a Spanish-speaking employee. You'll get better results if you can communicate with these employees in their own language. This chapter will teach you to speak the Spanish required to arrange hotel reservations and to make your hotel stay a pleasant one. You will learn how to request help unloading your luggage, getting it to your room, and making sure that everything in your room is in order. You will be able to request a taxi, and use the telephone to arrange for air or ground transportation.

Making Reservations

Reservations are a must for most hotels, particularly if you are planning on making your stay at a hotel a vacation. In this section, you learn the basic Spanish required to make hotel reservations.

Go to audio file 10a Making reservations.

You also learn how to ask about hotel amenities and the price of various types of rooms.

The following dialogue is presented in conversational form as though it takes place over the telephone:

Thank you for calling the Hotel Presidente. Can I help you?	*Gracias por llamar al Hotel Presidente. ¿En qué le puedo servir?*
I am looking for a nice hotel for my family's vacation.	*Busco un hotel agradable para la vacación de mi familia.*
Do you have a room available for June 28 through July 5?	*¿Tiene usted un cuarto disponible para el veintiocho de junio hasta el cinco de julio?*
Yes, we have a room available.	*Sí, tenemos un cuarto disponible.*
How many people are there in your group?	*¿Cuántas personas hay en su grupo?*
There are two adults.	*Hay dos adultos.*
Do you have a two-bedroom suite for four people?	*¿Tiene usted una suite de dos dormitorios para cuatro personas?*
What size beds do you need?	*¿Qué tamaño de camas necesita usted?*
We want a king-size bed and a full, or queen-size bed.	*Queremos una cama de tamaño extra y una cama de matrimonio o de tamaño de reina.*
Do you have a three-bedroom suite for five people?	*¿Tiene usted una suite de tres dormitorios para cinco personas?*

I want a king-size, a queen-size, and a full-size bed.	Quiero una cama de tamaño extra, una de tamaño de reina, y una de matrimonio.
No, we don't have that kind of room available.	No, no tenemos esa clase de cuarto disponible.
Yes, we do.	Sí, lo tenemos.
Do you wish for a smoking or non-smoking suite?	¿Desea usted una suite donde se permite fumar o una donde no se permite fumar?
We want a non-smoking suite.	Queremos una suite donde no se permite fumar.

Discussing the Hotel's Amenities

Go to audio file 10b The amenities.

The thing that will most impress us about a hotel's amenities is if the hotel provides us a better lifestyle than what we have at home. It does not matter how impressive the decor or how expensive the bedding is; if we aren't comfortable in the room we will not enjoy our stay at the hotel. In this section we describe the amenities commonly found in a luxury hotel. We provide you the translated text that demonstrates how you can ask about amenities when calling the hotel about reservations. You also can use this information if you later need to speak to the hotel staff about any deficiencies in any of the amenities provided.

What amenities does your hotel have?	¿Qué comodidades tiene su hotel?
Our hotel has many amenities for your enjoyment.	Nuestro hotel tiene muchas comodidades para su disfrute.
Our hotel has all the amenities found in a five-star hotel.	Nuestro hotel tiene todas las comodidades encontradas en un hotel de cinco estrellas.
They are all free for registered customers.	Todas ellas son gratis para clientes registrados.
The suite has two private bedrooms and a large living room.	La suite tiene dos dormitorios privados y una sala grande.

The suite has:	La suite tiene:
a microwave.	un horno de microondas.
a refrigerator.	un refrigerador.
air conditioning.	el aire acondicionado.
new pillow-top mattresses.	los colchones máximos en la almohada nuevos.
dual remote control electric blankets.	las mantas eléctricas con dos remotos de control.
lighted make-up mirror.	un espejo de maquillaje iluminado.
a three-speed hairdryer.	un secador para el pelo de tres velocidades.
an ironing board.	una tabla de planchar.
free newspaper.	el periódico gratis.
an automatic coffee maker.	una cafetera automática.
a reclining chair with a massager.	una silla recostable con un massager.
The rooms were recently carpeted.	Los cuartos fueron recientemente alfombrados.
The hotel has the following amenities for your enjoyment:	El hotel tiene las siguientes comodidades para su disfrute:
a 25-inch digital television set in each bedroom.	un televisor digital de veinticinco pulgadas en cada dormitorio.
a 32-inch digital television set in the living room.	un televisor digital de treinta y dos pulgadas en la sala.
cable tv.	una televisión cablegráfica.
in-room pay-per-view movies.	las películas de pague por vista en el cuarto.
high-speed Internet service.	el servicio de la internet de alta velocidad.
private balcony with panoramic view.	el balcón privado con vista panorámica.
parking with 24-hour security	el estacionamiento con seguridad de 24 horas.
valet parking.	el servicio de conducción al parqueo.
a swimming pool.	una piscina.
a jacuzzi.	un jacuzzi.

a spa.	*una spa.*
an exercise room.	*un cuarto de ejercicio.*
a sauna.	*un sauna.*
a tennis court.	*una cancha de tenis.*
a championship golf course.	*un campo de golf de campeonato.*

Inquiring About Rates

The phrases in this section will help you inquire about hotel rates. You can use these phrases to ask for hotel rates per night or by the week on single rooms and suites.

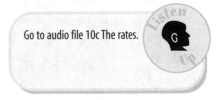

Go to audio file 10c The rates.

How much does the room cost per night?	*¿Cuánto cuesta el cuarto por noche?*
The rate is $100 per night.	*El precio es cien dólares por noche.*
How much does the two-bedroom suite cost per night?	*¿Cuánto cuesta la suite de dos dormitorios por noche?*
The rate is $150 per night.	*El precio es ciento cincuenta dólares por noche.*
What is the rate on the three-room suite?	*¿Cuál es el precio en la suite de tres cuartos?*
The rate is $175 per night.	*El precio es ciento setenta y cinco dólares por noche.*
Do you have weekly rates?	*¿Tiene usted precios semanales?*
You save 20% of the cost if you rent by the week.	*Usted ahorra veinte por ciento del costo si usted renta por semana.*
I want to reserve the two-bedroom suite for one week.	*Quiero reservar la suite de dos dormitorios por una semana.*
I need your name, address, and telephone number.	*Necesito su nombre, dirección, y el número de teléfono.*
We have reserved a two-bedroom suite for you for the week of June 29 through July 5 at $120 per night.	*Hemos reservado una suite de dos dormitorios para usted para la semana del veintinueve de junio al cinco de julio a ciento veinte dólares por noche.*
Your confirmation number is TBS120	*Su número de confirmación es TBS ciento veinte.*

Checking In

Checking in to a hotel is simple if you have reserved a room in advance. If you have not, then you have to go up to the counter and inquire about room availability (as you learned to do in the previous section of this chapter). In this section you learn phrases and sentences you can use to check in to a hotel without prior reservations, as well as those you can use when you have a confirmed reservation.

Go to audio file 10d
Checking in.

In this dialogue, two persons speak directly to each other:

May I help you?	*¿Le puedo ayudar?*
I want to rent a room.	*Quiero rentar un cuarto.*
Do you have reservations?	*¿Tiene usted reservaciones?*
No, I do not.	*No, no tengo.*
What size room do you need?	*¿Qué tamaño de cuarto necesita usted?*
I need a room with two double beds.	*Necesito un cuarto con dos camas dobles.*
How many nights do you plan to stay?	*¿Cuántas noches tiene intención de quedarse?*
I need the room for one night only.	*Necesito el cuarto por una noche solamente.*
How many people are there in your group?	*¿Cuántas personas hay en su grupo?*
There are two adults and one child.	*Hay dos adultos y un niño.*

In this dialog, a reservation has been made before check-in:

May I help you?	*¿Le puedo ayudar?*
Yes, I have a reservation.	*Sí, tengo una reservación.*
Do you have a confirmation number?	*¿Tiene usted un número de confirmación?*
Yes, I do.	*Sí, tengo.*
The confirmation number is TBS120.	*El número de confirmación es TBS ciento veinte.*
You have reserved a two-bedroom suite for one week.	*Usted ha reservado una suite de dos dormitorios por una semana.*
Please fill out the registration form.	*Por favor llene la forma de registración.*
How will you be paying for your stay?	*¿Cómo pagará usted su estadía?*
I will charge it to a credit card.	*Lo cargaré a una tarjeta de crédito.*

May I make an imprint of your card?	*¿Puedo hacer una impresión de su tarjeta?*
Here is your key to the suite.	*Aquí está su llave para la suite.*
Please call us if you need anything.	*Por favor llámenos si necesita cualquiera cosa.*

Asking for Bell Captain/Hop Assistance

The bell captain and bellhop can be a big help, if you are able to communicate to them what you need for them to do for you. In some hotels they are ready to serve you. They come out to your vehicle when you arrive. Sometimes a bellhop will get your luggage out of your vehicle and take it to the entrance of the hotel. Another bellhop will take your luggage to your room. You may have to tip both of them. In this section we will provide you material that you can use to get the assistance you require from the hotel attendants.

Go to audio file 10e Bellhop assistance.

May I help you, sir?	*¿Le puedo asistir, señor?*
May I help you, ma'am?	*¿Puedo ayudarle, señorita?*
Do you need assistance with your luggage?	*¿Necesita usted asistencia con su equipaje?*
Do you need assistance taking your luggage to your room?	*¿Necesita usted asistencia llevando su equipaje a su cuarto?*
I need help with my luggage.	*Necesito ayuda con mi equipaje.*
I wish to have my luggage taken to my room.	*Deseo que se lleve mi equipaje para mi cuarto.*
What is your room number?	*¿Qué es su número del cuarto?*
My room number is 245.	*El número de mi cuarto es doscientos cuarenta y cinco.*
I will follow you to my room.	*Le seguiré para mi cuarto.*
Do you wish for me to park your car?	*¿Desea que estacione su coche?*
Do you want me to park your car in the valet parking lot?	*¿Quiere usted que yo estacione su coche en el lote de servicio de conducción al parqueo?*
No, thank you, I will park it myself.	*No, gracias, lo estacionaré yo.*
Yes, please.	*Sí, por favor.*

Asking About Hotel Services

Go to audio file 10f Hotel services.

Hotels generally have brochures and other information about their services and things such as sightseeing tours that can make your stay more pleasant. This section provides phrases you can use to inquire about hotel services and any tours that may be available.

Is there anything that you need to know about our hotel?	*¿Hay cualquiera cosa que usted necesita saber acerca de nuestro hotel?*
Do you want a map?	*¿Quiere usted un mapa?*
Anything else?	*¿Algo más?*
I need more information on:	*Necesito más información sobre:*
the city.	*la ciudad.*
the restaurants.	*los restaurantes.*
the theaters.	*los teatros.*
the museums.	*los museos.*
sightseeing tours.	*las excursiones de visita a lugares de interés.*
This brochure describes our services.	*Este folleto describe nuestros servicios.*
Does the hotel have a safe-deposit box?	*¿Tiene el hotel una caja de seguridad?*
There is a safe in the walk-in closet of the bigger room.	*Hay una caja fuerte en el closet vestidor del cuarto mayor.*
Does the hotel have laundry service?	*¿Tiene el hotel servicio del lavandero?*
You can drop off your clothes here.	*Usted puede dejar sus ropas aquí.*
There is also a laundromat in the basement.	*Hay también una lavandería en el sótano.*
Do you provide room service for all meals?	*¿Provee usted servicio de habitaciones para todas las comidas?*
The hotel restaurant provides room service from 6:00AM to 11:00PM.	*El restaurante del hotel provee servicio de habitaciones desde las seis de la mañana hasta las once de la noche.*
There is a menu in your room.	*Hay un menú en su cuarto.*

Asking About Transportation and Auto Services Near the Hotel

Go to audio file 10g Public and private transportation.

During your hotel stay, you might need to use taxis, buses, and other forms of public transportation. You will almost certainly need some form of transportation to your hotel if you arrive at your destination city by air, train, or bus. You might want to attend a function where parking is an inconvenience, and it is best to take a taxi rather than drive your own vehicle. In this section you learn Spanish phrases you can use to inquire about available ground transportation, schedules, and location of the pick-up points or stations. This section also provides terms and sentences you can use to ask about gas stations and repair services for your private auto.

Does the Hotel Presidente have a shuttle service?	¿Tiene el Hotel Presidente un servicio regular de enlace?
There is shuttle, bus, subway, and taxi service available.	Hay servicio regular de enlace, autobús, metro, y servicio del taxi disponible.
Where can I catch a taxi?	¿Dónde puedo coger un taxi?
Here.	Aquí.
Over there.	Allá.
Across the street.	Al otro lado de la calle.
Where is the subway station?	¿Dónde está la estación del metro?
There is a subway two blocks from here.	Hay un metro dos bloques de aquí.
There is no subway in this area.	No hay metro en este área.
May I have a subway schedule?	¿Puedo tener un horario del metro?
There is a schedule in your room.	Hay un horario en su cuarto.
The parking lot trolley bus runs every hour on the half-hour.	El trolebús del estacionamiento corre cada hora en la media hora.
Where is the nearest gas station?	¿Dónde está la gasolinera próxima?
There is a gas station five blocks north of the hotel.	Hay una gasolinera cinco bloques al norte del hotel.
Where is the nearest auto garage?	¿Dónde está el taller mecánico del automóvil más cercano?
The closest dealership garage for your car is downtown.	El garaje del distribuidor para su coche más cercano está en el centro.

My car has a flat tire; where can I get it repaired?	¿Mi coche tiene una llanta desinflada; dónde la puedo reparar?
The gas station provides flat tire repair services.	La gasolinera provee servicios de reparación de la llanta desinflada.

Getting to the Airport from the Hotel

Go to audio file 10h Getting to the airport.

The phrases in this section will help you plan for your departure to the airport. You can use these phrases to get information on the location of the airport and to determine how long it will take you to reach the airport from your hotel:

How far is the airport from here?	¿Qué tan lejos está el aeropuerto de aquí?
It is about 15 miles.	Está cerca de quince millas.
How long does it take to get there from the hotel?	¿Cuánto tiempo se toma para llegar allí del hotel?
It takes 30 minutes during the low-traffic period.	Se toma treinta minutos durante el período de tráfico bajo.
It takes 1 hour and 45 minutes during rush hour traffic.	Se toma una hora y cuarenta y cinco minutos durante el tráfico de hora punta.

Reporting Problems with the Room

Go audio file 10i The room.

Earlier sections of this chapter provided you with sentences used to described the hotel room or suite and its accommodations (number of rooms and bed-sizes, and so on). In this section, you learn how to describe and report problems that you encounter in your room or suite.

This room is not what I requested.	Este cuarto no es lo que pedí.
This suite has the wrong size bed in one of the rooms.	Esta suite tiene una cama de tamaño incorrecto en uno de los cuartos.
The rooms are dirty.	Los cuartos están sucios.
The sliding door to the balcony does not lock.	La puerta corrediza para el balcón no traba.
The drapes do not close completely.	Las cortinas no se cierran completamente.

The elevator is too noisy.	El elevador es demasiado ruidoso.
The magnetic key does not work.	La llave magnética no opera.
The security lock is broken.	El cerrojo de seguridad está quebrado.
Please move us to another suite.	Por favor muévanos a otra suite.
We requested a non-smoking suite, and it smells as if someone smoked in it.	Pedimos una suite de no fumador, y huele como si alguien fumó en ella.
We will move you to a more luxurious suite at no additional cost to you.	Le moveremos a una suite más lujosa sin ningún costo adicional para usted.
If there is anything else wrong, let us know.	Si hay algo más mal, díganos.

Using the Telephone

In this section you will learn the Spanish expressions you can use to request information or services from the hotel staff over the telephone. This material will help you not only while on vacation; you'll also be able to use these sentences any time you speak with a Hispanic person or operator who does not speak English.

HELLO? HELLO?

Speaking of...

In the "Answering the Telephone" sidebar in the "Making an Appointment" section in Chapter 9, you learned that you may not get a "Hello" response from a Hispanic answering the telephone. You will probably get a response such as *Bueno?* or *Dígame*. Notice that even though "Hello" is not an interrogative, *Bueno* is because the respondent is asking "Well?" Next time you get a call from a Hispanic, answer the telephone by saying *Bueno?* These responses will be used in the telephone conversations illustrated in this section.

Hotels in some Latin American countries may not have direct dial capability. You may be required to go through an operator to make your long distance calls or even local calls. In the first part of this section we will help you make those kinds of calls.

When you dial the operator you may get one of the following two responses:

Go to audio file 10j Using the telephone.

Hello.	*¿Bueno?*
Hello.	*Dígame.*
Is this the hotel operator?	*¿Es ésta la operadora del hotel?*
Yes it is.	*Sí.*
I am trying to make a long distance call from my room.	*Trato de hacer una llamada de larga distancia de mi cuarto.*
I cannot get an outside line from my room.	*No puedo obtener una línea externa de mi cuarto.*
No, you cannot.	*No se puede.*
I will connect you to an outside line, then you can dial the number you want.	*Le haré conexión para una línea exterior, puede luego usted marcar el número que usted desea.*
I have to dial the number you want to call.	*Tengo que marcar el número que usted quiere llamar.*
Please dial 123-456-7890 for me.	*Por favor marque uno dos tres, cuatro cinco seis, setenta y ocho noventa para mí.*
That number is busy.	*Ese número está ocupado.*
I want to make a long-distance call.	*Quiero hacer una llamada de larga distancia.*
I want to make a collect call.	*Quiero hacer una llamadaa cobro revertido.*
I want to make a person-to-person call.	*Quiero hacer una llamada de persona a persona.*
I want to make a credit card call.	*Quiero hacer una llamada de la tarjeta de crédito.*

MY CELL PHONE DOES NOT WORK!

Communication is no problem in the U.S. We can call anywhere from anywhere on our cell phones. Unfortunately, our cell phones do not work in many Latin American countries where we might find ourselves on vacation. In fact, many countries do not even have direct dial capability. You have to go through an operator to make a telephone call. The material in this chapter will help you to make a telephone call using that system.

In many of the hotels you are able to dial the different hotel service providers directly from your hotel room. In others you may have to dial the operator. If that is the case, the Spanish phrases listed here will help you do that:

Please dial room 915.	*Por favor marque el cuarto novecientos quince.*
Please dial the dining room.	*Por favor marque por teléfono el comedor.*
I want to speak with the bell captain.	*Quiero hablar con el jefe de portería.*
Please dial the golf course.	*Por favor marque por teléfono el campo de golf.*
I want to make a tee time.	*Quiero hacer un horario de salida.*
Please dial the tennis court.	*Por favor marque por teléfono la cancha de tenis.*
Is the tennis court available at 6:00PM today?	*¿Está disponible la cancha de tenis a las seis de la tarde hoy?*

Summary

This chapter will prove to be very useful in making arrangements to stay at a hotel where the staff speaks Spanish. You will be able to check in and make sure that the room and all the hotel amenities meet your and your family's expectations. You learned how to request assistance, and arrange for ground or air transportation directly from the staff or over the telephone.

We take a new direction in the instruction we provide you in the next chapter. In Chapter 11, "Discussing Science and Computers," you learn phrases and sentences for discussing a variety of scientific topics, including natural sciences as well as computers, email, and other computer science topics.

Audio Files

Discussing Science and Computers

In this chapter you learn to talk about two very interesting subjects in very simple Spanish. In the first half of this chapter you will learn to talk about the natural world that surrounds us—nature, the weather, and non-human animals and insects with whom we share the planet. No heavy scientific terms here—instead, you learn how to discuss the natural world as anyone would in social conversation.

In the second half of this chapter, you learn how to discuss computers and computer technologies in Spanish. You learn terms and expressions useful for talking about computing on both laptop and desktop computers. You also learn Spanish terms, phrases, and expressions that will help you talk about using common software applications, accessing the Internet, and sending email.

Simple Conversations About Nature and Natural Sciences

You are unlikely to need to speak with your Hispanic friends, acquaintances, and coworkers about the molecular composition of a beautiful flower or the atomic

In this chapter:

* Participating in simple conversations about the natural world and natural sciences
* Discussing animals
* Talking about computers, software, the Internet, and email

structure of a stone. But you might want to talk with them about the natural world. Here, you learn sentences useful for casual conversations in Spanish about nature, the seasons, weather, animals, the color spectrum, and other things we can see, touch, smell, taste, and hear in the world around us.

Discussing Our Natural Environment

In this section we will talk about those things in nature that we so often take for granted, but enjoy very much when we notice them. In the following examples, the speakers are talking about a series of imaginary walks and the things they observed in nature:

Go to audio file 11a Nature.

Do you like to go for a walk?	*¿Le gusta dar un paseo?*
I enjoy going for a walk before dawn.	*Me gusta dar un paseo antes del amanecer.*
I get up early to see the sunrise.	*Madrugo para ver la salida del sol.*
The flowers are blooming.	*Las flores florecen.*
I love to see the cloud formations.	*Me gusta ver las formaciones de nubes.*
When it rained yesterday, I saw a rainbow.	*Cuando llovió ayer, vi un arco iris.*
I enjoy going for a walk in the cool of the evening.	*Me gusta ir de paseo en la calma de la tarde.*
I love to see the colors of the sunset.	*Me gusta ver los colores de la puesta de sol.*
You can see the sun reflected on the water.	*Usted puede ver el sol reflejado en el agua.*
At night you can see the stars in the sky.	*Por la noche usted puede ver las estrellas en el cielo.*
Look! You can see some planets.	*¡Mira! Puedes ver unos planetas.*
I saw a comet with a long tail.	*Vi un cometa con una cola larga.*
I like going to the park.	*Me gusta ir al parque.*
In the park I can lie under a tree and watch the clouds go by.	*En el parque puedo acostarme bajo de un árbol y mirar las nubes que pasan.*
I like walking in the desert.	*Me gusta caminar en el desierto.*
It is especially beautiful when the yuccas are in bloom.	*Es especialmente bello cuando los itabos están en flor.*
I like walking in the mountains.	*Me gusta caminar en las montañas.*

In the mountains you can see:	En las montañas usted puede ver:
rock formations.	las formaciones rocosas.
tall pine trees.	los pinos altos.
snow.	la nieve.

Talking About the Seasons

In this section, you learn how to state the dates when summer, winter, spring, and autumn begin. This section also provides some brief examples of sentences used in casual conversation about the seasons.

Go to audio file 11b Seasons.

Spring begins on March twenty-first.	La primavera empieza el veintiuno de marzo.
Summer begins on June twenty-second.	El verano empieza el veintidós de junio.
Autumn begins on September twenty-third.	El otoño empieza el veintitrés de septiembre.
Winter begins on December twenty-first.	El invierno empieza el veintiuno de diciembre.
Which is your favorite season?	¿Cuál es su estación favorita?
My favorite season is spring.	Mi estación favorita es la primavera.
The temperatures are moderate in the spring.	Las temperaturas son moderadas en la primavera.
The flowers bloom in the spring.	Las flores florecen en la primavera.
I like to go swimming in the summer.	Me gusta nadar en el verano.
I like to go fishing at the lake and river.	Me gusta ir de pesca en el lago y el río.
My favorite time of the year is the fall.	Mi tiempo favorito del año es el otoño.
I like to see the leaves on the trees changing colors.	Me gusta ver las hojas en los árboles cambiando colores.
My favorite season is winter.	Mi estación favorita es el invierno.
I like to go ice skating in the frozen ponds.	Me gusta ir al patinaje sobre hielo en los estanques congelados.
I go to the forest and chop wood for our fireplace.	Voy al bosque y corto la leña en trozos para nuestra chimenea.

Casual Conversations About Weather

It is amazing how much the subject of weather dominates our conversation. If we get on the phone with someone from across the country we ask them, "How's the weather?" Our electronic mail includes a description of the pleasant temperatures or lousy weather we have been having.

Go to audio file 11c Weather.

You can use these sentences to talk about the weather, in Spanish:

What is the weather like?	*¿Qué tiempo hace?*
The weather is nice.	*Hace buen tiempo.*
The weather is bad.	*Hace mal tiempo.*
A tornado was sighted three miles outside of town.	*Un tornado fue visto tres millas fuera de la ciudad.*
A hurricane destroyed many homes.	*Un huracán destruyó muchas casas.*
We had a hailstorm that dropped baseball-sized hail.	*Tuvimos una granizada que dejó caer granizo el tamaño de una béisbol.*
The heavy rain caused flooding downtown.	*La lluvia fuerte causó anegación en el centro.*
It is cold.	*Hace frío.*
It is below zero.	*Está bajo de cero.*
It is 2 degrees Celsius.	*Está a dos grados centígrado.*
It is hot.	*Hace calor.*
The temperature outside is 106 degrees.	*La temperatura de afuera está a ciento seis grados.*

Describing Colors and the Color Spectrum

Colors play an important part in our lives, and many discussions include references to colors or color combinations. In this section, you will find a list of some of the more common colors. The list

Go to audio file 11d Colors.

will be followed by phrases that teach you how the form of the color changes with the number and gender of what is being described. The phrases will include colors not on the list.

Here is a list of common colors:

red	rojo
blue	azul
white	blanco
gray	gris
brown	marrón
pink	rosado
green	verde
turquoise	turquesa
violet	violeta
mauve	malva
lavender	espliego
silver	plata
gold	oro

The following phrases show you how the colors agree with the nouns they describe in number and gender.

I use a piece of black coal as a paperweight.	Uso un pedazo de carbón negro como un pisapapeles.
I received two black pearl necklaces from Tahiti.	Recibí dos collares de perlas negras de Tahiti.
He gave her a yellow canary.	Él le dio a ella un canario amarillo.
He gave her a dozen yellow roses.	él le dio a ella una docena de rosas amarillas.
An orange-colored bird came to our bird feeder.	Un pájaro anaranjado vino a nuestro alimentador del pájaro.
I saw two orange-colored butterflies in the flower bed.	Vi a dos mariposas anaranjadas en el macizo de flores.

Discussing Wildlife

In this section of the chapter, you learn conversational Spanish that you can use to talk about animals. You can use this material to talk to Hispanic children and adults about birds and other animals you see on television, at the zoo, and in wildlife parks.

SPEAKING OF ANIMALS

In the "Pets" section of Chapter 5, "Talking About Your Town, Home, and Personal Belongings," we listed some animals that are kept as pets. Technically, any animal that is domesticated can be called a pet. In this chapter, however, we talk about a wide range of birds and animals, including domesticated animals.

Talking About Animals

You don't have to live in the African veldt or a South American rainforest to see a vast number of wild animals. You need only visit a zoo, a wild animal park, or a safari to see exotic wildlife. And entire television channels are now devoted to animals, giving us plenty to talk about as we discuss the domestic and wild animals that share our planet.

Here are some examples of sentences you might use when talking about animals:

Have you gone to a zoo?	*¿Tú has ido a un zoológico?*
We visited a wild animal park in Florida.	*Visitamos un parque de animales salvajes en la Florida.*
What animals did you see?	*¿Qué animales viste tú?*
I saw:	*Vi:*
a large elephant.	*un elefante grande.*
a hippopotamus.	*un hipopótamo.*
a gorilla.	*una gorila.*
a chimpanzee.	*un chimpancé.*
some monkeys.	*unos monos.*
A lion.	*un león.*
a wolf.	*un lobo.*
a black leopard.	*un leopardo negro.*

tip The television can take us to zoos, nature parks, and wild natural locations that are home to a vast array of wildlife. The TV also provides an excellent opportunity to use the material in this section to teach children the Spanish names of a number of wild and domesticated animals.

Go to audio file 11e Animals.

a cheetah.	un guepardo.
a gazelle.	una gacela.
an antelope.	un antílope.
three grizzly bears.	tres osos pardos.
a whale.	una ballena.
a zebra.	una cebra.

Discussing Birds

Go to audio file 11f Birds.

The Spanish sentences you learn in this section describe a variety of birds and their distinctive characteristics.

I went to a bird sanctuary.	Fui a un santuario de pájaros.
I enjoy watching TV programs about birds.	Me gusta mirar programas de televisión que exhiben a los pájaros.
The robins have returned to our town.	Los petirrojos han regresado a nuestro pueblo.
I enjoy watching birds.	Me gusta mirar los pájaros.
I have a birdfeeder in my yard.	Tengo un comedero del pájaro en mi patio.
The finches and cardinals have such bright feathers!	¡Los pinzones y cardenales tienen unas plumas tan brillantes!
In summer, I wake up early to the chirping of the birds.	En el verano, me despierto temprano al gorjear de los pájaros.
The Mexican restaurant had a parrot that talked.	El restaurante mejicano tenía un perico que hablaba.
The parrot had green feathers, and a red and yellow head.	El perico tenía plumas verdes, y una cabeza roja y amarilla.
I love to hear the mockingbirds sing.	Me gusta oír a los sinsontes cantar.
The pink flamingos have long legs and a hooked beak.	Los flamencos rosados tienen patas largas y un pico de ave ganchudo.
We have a hummingbird feeder close to our window.	Tenemos un alimentador del colibrí cerca de nuestra ventana.
I enjoyed seeing the colorful feathers of the macaw.	Me dio gusto ver las plumas coloridas del guacamayo.

Talking About Computers

The personal computer has come into everybody's life, including the most modest homes. Even those of us who don't have computers at home are exposed to computers any time we go to a department store, bank, insurance office, or a local, state, or federal government office to transact business. Our children get to use computers in school. Because computers are such an integral part of our lives today, discussions about them and their use are frequently part of our business and casual conversations.

This section describes computer hardware characteristics and capabilities that apply to both desktop and laptop computers. Here, you learn to describe and discuss the use of both types of computer and common types of software. You also learn simple sentences for discussing accessing the Internet and using email.

THIS ISN'T A TECHNICAL MANUAL!

Computers are complex machines that are difficult to understand. They are even more difficult to describe in simple conversational terms. In this chapter, we don't waste your time by quoting from technical manuals; most technical manuals come in all languages, including Spanish. The intent of the material in this section is to provide you the translated conversational Spanish for some of the questions that may be asked by someone who simply wants to use—not build—a computer. The responses are in terms that any person can understand.

Common Computer Tasks and Features

Though desktop and laptop computers have different physical features, they are used to do the same types of tasks. Desktop and laptop computers have similar processing capabilities, so the following examples apply to the use of both types of computer.

Go to audio file 11g Talking about computers.

Do you own a personal computer?	*¿Tienes una computadora personal?*
Yes, I own a personal computer.	*Sí, tengo una computadora personal.*
No, I do not own a computer.	*No, no tengo una computadora.*

Are you going to buy a new computer?	¿Vas a comprar una computadora nueva?
I plan to buy a computer.	Tengo intención de comprar una computadora.
How much memory does your computer have?	¿Cuánta memoria tiene tu computadora?
My computer has lots of memory and a large hard disk.	Mi computadora tiene mucha memoria y un disco duro extenso.
I have a Technon with Pentium 4 microprocessor.	Tengo un Technon con un microprocesador Pentium cuatro.
My Technon has a 2.6 gigahertz memory.	Mi Technon tiene memoria de dos punto seis gigahertz.
Is your computer fast?	¿Es rápida tu computadora?
It is super-fast.	Es superrápida.
Did it cost a lot of money?	¿Costó mucho dinero?
It cost less than $1,000.	Costó menos de mil dólares.

THE COMPUTER'S GENDER

Talking Points

You will hear Hispanics refer to the computer as either *la computadora* (female gender), or *el computador* (male gender). It is acceptable to use either term in the Americas. Both terms are used throughout this book. The only requirement is that the appropriate gender be applied to the term selected. A computer is referred to as *el ordenador* (male gender), or the "ordainer" in Spain.

I use my computer to:	Uso mi computadora para:
type and store documents.	escribir y almacenar documentos.
perform calculations.	realizar cálculos.
prepare spreadsheets.	preparar hojas contables.
download, use, or store data from the Internet.	bajar a disco, usar, o almacenar datos de la Internet.
download digital images from a camera, scanner, or the Internet.	bajar a disco imágenes digitales de una cámara, un escáner, o la Internet.

edit photos and other images.	editar fotos y otras imágenes.
store digital images.	almacenar imágenes digitales.
print photos and documents.	imprimir fotos y documentos.
I use a Desktop computer at work.	Uso una computadora de escritorio en el trabajo.
My desktop has a 21-inch monitor.	Mi computadora de escritorio tiene un monitor de veintiuna pulgadas.
I own a laptop computer.	Tengo una computadora portátil.
I can do anything on my laptop that I could do on a desktop computer.	Puedo hacer cualquiera cosa en mi computadora portátil que podría hacer en una computadora de escritorio.
The advantage of a laptop is portability	La ventaja de una computadora portátil es la portabilidad.
My laptop weighs around 6 pounds.	Mi computadora portátil pesa más o menos seis libras.
The laptop can operate up to two hours on a battery.	La computadora portátil puede funcionar hasta dos horas con una batería.

note A laptop computer is sometimes referred to as a notebook. Laptop and notebook computers are both called *una computadora portátil* in Spanish. *Portátil* means portable.

COMPUTER TALK

Talking Points

Talk about a universal language—computer talk may be it. Many English computer terms are used by Hispanics without the benefit of translation. You will notice that throughout this chapter many of the words related to computers are not translated. They do get the Spanish inflection when pronounced. Here is a sampling of these words: software, Internet, Ethernet, email, chat, CD-ROM, RAM, joystick, link, megabyte, Web, and microchip. Not all of these words are used in this chapter.

Conversations About the Use of Software

In this section we are going to talk about software in very general terms. Social conversation does not generally get into details about what software runs the operating system or applications in a computer. This section includes Spanish sentences you can use to describe some software and its capabilities. You also learn expressions useful for discussing how to compose, edit, and store documents, and how to develop multi-functional spreadsheets.

Go to audio file 11h Software.

Software provides the instruction that tells the computer what to do.	*El software provee la instrucción que le dice a la computadora que hacer.*
I use word processing software, a spreadsheet program, and presentation	*Uso software de procesamiento de texto, un programa de la hoja contable, y software de presentación.*
You can type documents and develop spreadsheets, among other things.	*Usted puede escribir documentos y puede desarrollar hojas contables, entre otras cosas.*
Word processing software allows you to compose, edit, and print documents.	*El software de procesamiento de texto le permite componer, editar, e imprimir documentos.*
Spreadsheet software allows you to sort and calculate numbers	*El software de la hoja contable te permite ordenar y calcular números.*
I can't find my document.	*No puedo hallar mi documento.*
You can search for your document by name.	*Puedes buscar tu documento por el nombre.*
Did you create a folder for your document?	*¿Creaste una carpeta para tu documento?*
You need to run the spellcheck on this letter.	*Necesitas ejecutar el corrector ortográfico en esta carta.*
Can you show me how to create a mailing list with this program?	*¿Me puedes enseñar como crear una lista de correo con este programa?*
Do you know how to use a spreadsheet program?	*¿Sabes como usar un programa de la hoja contable?*
I can use a spreadsheet program to do basic calculations.	*Puedo usar un programa de la hoja contable para hacer cálculos básicos.*

Talking About the Internet

Go to audio file 11i Internet.

The Internet is a much-discussed topic. These sample sentences are useful for describing what the Internet is and what it can be used for:

Do you use the Internet often?	*¿Usas la Internet a menudo?*
You have to sign up with an Internet service provider to access the Internet.	*Tú tienes que alistarte con un proveedor de servicio de la Internet para obtener acceso a la Internet.*
How do you access a site on the Internet?	*¿Cómo obtienes acceso a un sitio en la Internet?*
You access it by clicking on its hyperlink.	*Tú obtienes acceso dando un clic sobre su hiperenlace.*
You need a web browser to access the World Wide Web.	*Tú necesitas un navegador de Web para tener acceso a la Red Mundial.*
You can research any subject online.	*Tú puedes investigar cualquier tema en linea.*
What kind of a modem do you use?	*¿Qué clase del modem usas?*
I have a broadband connection.	*Tengo una conexión de la banda ancha.*
I use a DSL connection.	*Uso una conexión del DSL.*
I have a dial-up connection and modem.	*Tengo una conexión por la línea conmutada y módem.*
I read the online version of my local newspaper.	*Leo la versión en línea de mi periódico local.*
I search for jobs online using a search engine, such as Google.	*Busco trabajos en línea usando un motor de búsqueda, como Google.*
I do a lot of my shopping online.	*Hago muchas de mis compras en línea.*
I have my own Website; the address is www.mysite.com.	*Tengo mi propio sitio web; la dirección es www.mysite.com.*

Exchanging Information About Email

Go to audio file 11j Email.

Electronic mail is one of the more significant benefits of the computer. It's fast and effective in transmitting documents or graphics, and it's a great way to stay in touch with friends, relatives, and business associates.

In the following sample sentences, the parties are talking about using email:

Do you use email?	*¿Usas el correo electrónico?*
Do you have an email address?	*¿Tienes una dirección del correo electrónico?*
You can chat with someone by using instant messaging.	*Tú puedes platicar con alguien usando envío de mensajes instantáneos.*
Why would I need to set up an email account?	*¿Por qué necesitaría establecer una cuenta del correo electrónico?*
My ISP (Internet service provider) is having problems with its server.	*Mi ISP (el proveedor del servicio de la Internet) tiene problemas con su servidor.*
How do I set up an email account?	*¿Cómo establezco una cuenta del correo electrónico?*
Contact your ISP and request that they set up an email account for you.	*Contacta tu proveedor del servicio de la Internet y pide que establezcan una cuenta del correo electrónico para ti.*
What is your email address?	*¿Cuál es tu dirección del correo electrónico?*
Please send me that information in an email message.	*Por favor envíame esa información en un mensaje del correo electrónico.*
My email address is Annamarie@myemail.com.	*Mi dirección del correo electrónico es Annamarie@myemail.com.*
I never open up email attachments, if I don't know the sender.	*Nunca abro adjuntos del correo electrónico, si no conozco al remitente.*
Did your computer get infected with the latest virus?	*¿Se infectó tu computadora con el último virus?*
I use anti-virus software to check email attachments.	*Uso software de antivirus para revisar adjuntos del correo electrónico.*

Summary

In this chapter we talked about the natural world, natural sciences, and computers—subjects that can be very dry if discussed strictly in technical terms. Instead, you learned terms and phrases useful for discussing these topics in a simple conversational mode. We provided you with Spanish you can use to talk about the beauty of nature, the seasons, weather, and the colors of the color spectrum. We also provided conversations about a variety of animals and birds, their characteristics, and habitat.

This chapter also included a number of translated sentences you'll find useful when talking about computers, software, the Internet, and email. In the next chapter we will be talking about the business world, including retail and investment business processes, legal services, and Spanish advertising in the media.

Audio Files

- [ ] 12a Auto sales
- [ ] 12b Real estate sales
- [ ] 12c Investments
- [ ] 12d Legal services
- [ ] 12e Advertising legal services
- [ ] 12f Advertising in the newspaper
- [ ] 12g Advertising on the radio
- [ ] 12h Advertising on the Internet

12

In this chapter:

- ✳ Discussing auto and real estate sales and investments
- ✳ Discussing legal matters
- ✳ Advertising in newspapers, radio, television, and the Internet

The Professional World

There are hundreds of businesses we could talk about in a chapter with a title like "The Professional World." In this chapter, we include a number of discussions relating to business transactions in the auto, real estate, and investments markets. Here, you learn how to discuss goods and services available in each of these markets, as well as some key phrases and sentences for closing sales and investments.

This chapter also provides some sentences useful for seeking and discussing legal services. The final sections of the chapter are devoted to advertising, to help you put together some basic advertising copy that will be useful for reaching Hispanics through newspapers, radio, and the Internet.

Discussing Auto Sales, Real Estate, and Investments

There are many ways to let people know about the products and services you provide. You can send potential customers a letter, a flyer, or an email, if you know their address. You can place signs inside and outside your business, or along the highway. You can establish a website for your business on the Internet, or put an ad on someone else's website. Finally, you can advertise in the newspaper, the radio, or television. There are many ways to tell the world about your products and services. The important thing is to make sure people understand why they need your product. You must communicate at their level. If you are not talking to Hispanics in their native language, you are probably not reaching them. This chapter will help you convey your message to them. They are, after all, the largest minority group in the U.S. and a lucrative market.

HISPANICS—THE LARGEST MINORITY IN THE U.S.

According to Census Bureau Director Louis Kincannon, in a press release dated June 18, 2003, "The official population estimates now indicate that the Hispanic community is the nation's largest minority community." This information is available at the following URL: http://www.census.gov/Press-Release/www/2003/cb03-100.html

Discussing an Automobile Purchase

After we buy a car, we like to talk about how we totally "stole the car" from the salesperson (even though we secretly worry that the salesperson is getting high fives from his cohorts for finding such easy money). In this section we will describe the process of purchasing an auto, including the search, negotiation, and purchase processes. We will include questions that you as a salesperson may get from Hispanic customers interested in buying an auto.

Advertising Car Sales

If you want to place banners on your lot announcing a sale, here are some suggestions for ways you might word those advertisements:

Go to audio file 12a Auto sales.

End of Year Sale.	La Venta de Fin de Año.
Inventory Reduction Sale.	La Venta de Reducción de Inventario.
Memorial Day Sale.	La Venta del Día Memorial.
Independence Day Sale.	La Venta del Día de la Independencia.
4th of July Sale.	La Venta del cuatro de julio.

Meeting and Greeting Customers at the Car Dealership

You can greet Hispanic customers and then ask them how you can help them using the following sentences:

Welcome to our showroom.	Bienvenido a nuestra sala de exhibición.
Welcome to our car lot.	Bienvenido a nuestro lote de autos.
What car are you looking for?	¿Qué coche busca usted?
I am looking for a used car.	Busco un coche usado.
I want to buy a new car.	Quiero comprar un coche nuevo.
I am looking for an economy car.	Busco un coche económico.
I am looking for a mid-sized car.	Busco un coche de tamaño mediano.
We need a 4-door car.	Necesitamos un coche de cuatro puertas.
We are interested in an SUV.	Estamos interesados en un vehículo utilitario deportivo.
I have exactly what you are looking for.	Tengo exactamente lo que usted busca.
I have a new car that has:	Tengo un coche nuevo que tiene:
I have a low-mileage car that has:	Tengo un coche de millaje bajo que tiene:
automatic transmission.	la transmisión automática.
air conditioning.	el aire acondicionado.
leather seats.	los asientos forrados en piel.
AM/FM stereo radio with CD player.	la radio AM/FM estérea con el reproductor de CD.
power windows.	los vidrios eléctricos.
power locks.	cierre central de puertas.
alarm system.	el sistema de alarma.
Are you interested in buying it?	¿Tiene interés usted en comprarlo?
I'll buy it.	Lo compraré.
Do you have a trade-in?	¿Tiene usted un intercambio?
Can you give a $1,000 down-payment?	¿Puede dar usted un desembolso inicial de mil dólares?
Do you want for us to arrange for financing your purchase?	¿Quiere usted que nosotros hagamos los preparativos para financiar su compra?
No, I am not ready to buy yet.	No, no estoy listo para comprar todavía.

Discussing Real Estate Sales

Go to audio file 12b Real estate sales

A critical element in selling real estate is matching your customer's need to what you have to offer. Purchasing a home can be an emotional experience for a first-time buyer. The sale may require more "sales pitch" than for someone who has gone through a couple of purchases. To make your customer feel comfortable and confident, you have to convince the customer that you are a friend there to help him or her, not an insensitive salesperson.

note See Chapter 2, "Letters, Numbers, Dates, and Dollars," to practice translating specific numbers and dollar amounts. The information in this chapter will also help you in scheduling dates and times for viewing homes. Chapter 5, "Talking About Your Town, Home, and Personal Belongings," includes terms and phrases you'll find useful for describing various rooms within a home.

To refresh your skills in basic greetings and small talk, review Chapter 3, "Getting to Know One Another." Getting to know your customer requires that you ask a lot of questions. The answer to many of the questions will be a yes or no, or some unique response such as the name of the city where your customer is moving in from. We will not provide those kinds of answers. In these sample sentences, we provide more detailed responses:

What kind of house are you looking for?	¿Qué clase de casa busca?
Do you currently own a home?	¿Es usted dueño actualmente de una casa?
Are you preapproved for a loan at a certain amount?	¿Ha sido usted preaprobado para un préstamo a cierta cantidad?
How many bedrooms do you need?	¿Cuántas recámaras necesita usted?
What price range are you looking for?	¿Más o menos qué precio busca usted?
Do you want a house with a living room and a den or family room?	¿Quiere usted una casa con una sala y un estudio o un cuarto familiar?
Do you want a house with a swimming pool?	¿Quiere usted una casa con una piscina?
Do you want to move to a specific neighborhood?	¿Quiere usted mudarse a un barrio específico?
I want a house:	Quiero una casa:
with two bedrooms.	con dos recámaras.
with three bedrooms.	con tres recámaras.
with a family room.	con un cuarto familiar.

close to an elementary school.	*cerca de una escuela primaria.*
close to a middle school.	*cerca de una escuela de ciclo medio.*
close to the shopping mall.	*cerca del centro comercial.*
close to the hospital.	*cerca del hospital.*

If you have the house or property the customer is looking for, you can state the following:

I have just the house for you.	*Tengo precisamente la casa para usted.*
I have exactly what you are looking for.	*Tengo exactamente lo que usted busca.*
I have a two-bedroom condominium I want to show you.	*Tengo un condominio de dos recámaras que quiero mostrarle.*
I have a three-bedroom house with:	*Tengo una casa de tres recámaras con:*
a basement.	*un sótano.*
three bathrooms.	*tres cuartos de baño.*
a vaulted ceiling in the living room.	*un cielo abovedado en la sala.*
a family room on the second floor.	*un cuarto familiar en el segundo piso.*
a three-car attached garage.	*un garaje de tres coches adjunto.*
all new appliances.	*todos los aparatos nuevos.*
The house can be seen at 1:00PM this Saturday.	*La casa puede ser vista a la una de la tarde este sábado.*

If it appears that your customer is interested in looking at the house, you may want to provide him or her with a handout. If possible, you should have the handout information translated into Spanish. The following will help you talk to your prospective client about the handout.

Speaking of...

This section includes a limited description of what is in a house. The "Details of Your House" section in Chapter 5 provides a description of the various rooms in a house. It also provides details on fixtures, appliances, and other information you can use to describe what is in the house you are trying to sell.

This handout provides you information on:	*Esta hoja suelta le provee información en:*
the address of the house.	*la dirección de la casa.*
the room sizes.	*el tamaño de los cuartos.*
the lot size.	*el tamaño del lote.*
zoning restrictions.	*las restricciones de zonificación.*
estimated property taxes.	*los impuestos sobre bienes estimados.*
estimated home insurance cost.	*el costo de seguro de casa estimado.*

Making Investments

Investments come in many forms. A bank, savings and loan company, or a brokerage firm can provide investment services. The services that a potential customer might seek can range from

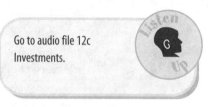

Go to audio file 12c
Investments.

opening a savings account to establishing a college education fund or retirement account. The material in this section is presented from the investment manager's viewpoint. We will provide material you can use to guide investors through the process of talking about options, setting up an account, and making deposits to and withdrawing from an account.

The following sample sentences describe a discussion between an investment counselor and a walk-in customer:

May I help you?	*¿Le puedo asistir?*
What are my investment options?	*¿Qué son mis opciones inversoras?*
How can I save for retirement?	*¿Cómo puedo ahorrar para el retiro?*
How can I save for my children's education?	*¿Cómo puedo ahorrar para la educación de mis niños?*
You can invest:	*Usted puede invertir:*
in a savings account.	*en una cuenta de ahorros.*
in an IRA account.	*en una cuenta IRA.*
in the stock market.	*en la bolsa de valores.*
What do they provide?	*¿Qué proveen?*
A savings account pays interest on the amount deposited.	*Una cuenta de ahorros paga interés en la cantidad depositada.*
You pay tax on the interest earned.	*Usted paga impuesto en el interés devengado.*
An IRA account pays interest on the amount invested.	*Una cuenta IRA paga interés en la cantidad invertida.*

You can invest $3,000 per person annually.	Usted puede invertir tres mil dólares por persona anualmente.
The annual investment is tax-deferred.	La inversión anual es diferida en impuesto.
You can buy shares in a company.	Usted puede comprar partes en una compañía.
You earn dividends if the company makes a profit.	Usted gana dividendos si la compañía gana dinero.
Dividends are taxable.	Los dividendos son gravables.
I want to invest in the stock market.	Quiero invertir dinero en la bolsa de valores.

Talking About Legal Matters

If this were an ideal world, we would never have to deal with legal matters. If we all got along with each other and never had any disagreements, or if we lived in world without so many rules, there would be no legal issues to resolve. The fact is that we do not always get along with each other and we do have disagreements and conflict. Furthermore, we live in a society with so many rules that it is difficult to go through life without breaking any. Consequently, we need the legal profession's help in resolving these legal matters. In this section we will describe the services that lawyers provide. We will then provide translations that the legal profession can use to advertise their services in the newspaper, phone directory, and magazines.

Discussing Legal Services

It seems as though everything we do requires the services of an attorney. There are so many laws that control every aspect of our lives that we sometimes feel as though we cannot or should not move without the advice of a lawyer.

Go to audio file 12d Legal services.

There will be no lawyer bashing or razzing in this section. They can save us a lot of grief when we get in trouble. The problem lies in determining what kind of lawyer we need for a situation we find ourselves embroiled in. It may be a good idea to go through a lawyer referral service. The minimal fee charged may save you a larger sum of money. We have to remember that for lawyers, time is money. We must have done our homework and have all documents in order when we go in to see them.

The first part of our discussion will address the services that the law offices provide. The functional description of the service will be presented in a presumed conversation between a customer and the law office employee or lawyer.

The following sample sentences are customer statements describing the customer's legal issue or needs:

I was involved in an auto accident and my insurance refuses to pay for my personal injuries.	*Estuve involucrado en un accidente del automóvil y mi seguro se rehúsa a pagar mis lesiones personales.*
There was discrimination against me.	*Hubo discriminación contra mi.*
I suffered back and neck injuries in a forklift accident.	*Sufrí lesiones de la espalda y del cuello en un accidente de la carretilla elevadora.*
My mother broke her hip when she fell at a store.	*Mi mamá se fracturó la cadera cuando se cayó en una tienda.*
I have worked in the U.S. for 45 years and now the government is trying to deport me.	*He trabajado en los EEUU por cuarenta y cinco años y ahora el gobierno intenta deportarme.*
I need help in filling out an insurance form.	*Necesito ayuda en llenar una forma de seguro.*

These statements tell customers what the legal service can do to accommodate their needs:

One of our paralegals will help you fill out the form.	*Uno de nuestros paralegales le ayudará a llenar la forma.*
It appears that you have a legitimate case.	*Parece que usted tiene un caso legítimo.*
You have a valid complaint.	*Usted tiene una queja válida.*
One of our attorneys specializes in cases similar to yours.	*Uno de nuestros abogados se especializa en los casos parecidos al suyo.*
An attorney consultation can help you decide if you want to pursue this case.	*Una consulta del abogado le puede ayudar a decidirse si usted quiere seguir adelante con este caso.*
Our attorney consultation fee is $35.	*Nuestro precio de consulta del abogado es treinta y cinco dólares.*
We will provide you with a free consultation.	*Le proveeremos con una consulta gratis.*

Advertising Legal Services

In 1977, the Supreme Court rendered the decision that lawyers could advertise. Unfortunately, much of the advertising is strictly in English, and does not reach non-English speaking Hispanic people.

Go to audio file 12e
Advertising legal services.

Spanish language ads can be more effective in reaching non–English-speaking Hispanics. Hispanics have a higher regard for businesses that make an effort to communicate with them in their native language. You should make every effort to have your Spanish ads professionally done. If your ads include audio, make sure that you use Spanish-speaking talent to present them. You have to let Hispanics know that you are equipped to help solve their legal problems.

In this section we provide you some slogans that you can use to advertise your services in the newspaper. If any of the following slogans or advertising lines are similar to an actual ad, it is a pure coincidence. We did not copy any law firm's slogan or advertisement. We also provide you conversational text that you can use to interview Hispanic customers who come into your office to try to determine what their legal needs are.

Come see us if you need a:	*Venga a vernos si usted necesita un:*
lawyer.	*abogado.*
law adviser.	*asesor jurídico.*
legal adviser.	*abogado consultor.*
civil lawyer.	*abogado civilista.*
criminal lawyer.	*abogado penalista.*
defense lawyer.	*abogado defensor.*
labor lawyer.	*abogado laborista.*
Our office is staffed with qualified lawyers.	*Nuestra oficina cuenta con abogados titulados.*
Come see us for all your legal needs.	*Venga a vernos para todas sus necesidades de curso legal.*
If you have suffered personal injury from a vehicle accident, we can help you.	*Si usted ha sufrido lesión personal de un accidente del vehículo, le podemos ayudar.*
If you were injured on the job and are having difficulty collecting Workers compensation, please call us.	*Si usted fue lastimado en el trabajo y tiene dificultad colectando compensación de trabajadores, por favor llámenos.*
We specialize in Business law, Real estate, and Commercial law.	*Nos especializamos en el Derecho Mercantil, Bienes Raíces, y Código de Comercio.*
We guarantee results.	*Garantizamos resultados.*
Get on a winning team.	*Póngase en un equipo ganador.*
Call us at 111-800-3456.	*Llámenos en uno, uno, uno, ochocientos, treinta y cuatro, cincuenta y seis.*
Come see us at 123 Main, Any City, State.	*Venga a vernos en uno dos tres Main, Cualquiera Ciudad, Estado.*

| We are on your side, call us at 111-800-3456. | Estamos en su lado, llámenos por teléfono en uno, uno, uno, ochocientos, treinta y cuatro, cincuenta y seis. |
| We take cases on a contingency basis. | Tomamos casos a contingencia. |

Advertising in the Media

The media provides the means to let people know what is going on in the nation and the local community, in addition to providing information on things of local interest, such as entertainment programming. It is an exceptional way to tell consumers about the products and services that your business offers. National, state, and local governments use the media to inform the public about new programs being implemented. Everybody is exposed to information provided in the newspaper, radio, television, or the Internet. An eye-catching ad can reap great benefits for a business. In this section you are provided phrases that are found in all forms of advertising.

The fact is that American business advertising in Spanish radio and television is limited. The only ones that seem to advertise on Mexican TV are the lawyers. Hispanic purchasing power should not be ignored. It would make sense for the business world and the media to work together to try to reach the Hispanic market.

HISPANIC PURCHASING POWER

In a recent research item released by the Hispanic Association on Corporate Responsibility, the Hispanic purchasing power in the U.S. was $630 billion in 2002.

This item appeared at http://www.hacr.org/statistics.htm.

Creating Newspaper Ads

The newspaper is a relatively inexpensive medium that can be used to reach potential customers. Many Hispanic households have at least one individual who reads English and will therefore subscribe to the newspaper. Hispanics are very interested in learning to read English. They will pick up the newspaper and glance through. Advertising in Spanish will definitely catch their eye. In this section we provide general phrases that can be used by a grocery store and a service provider to build an ad. We also provide examples of ad copy for four different types of businesses.

Go to audio file 12f
Advertising in the newspaper.

The following phrases provide a sampling of ads that can be placed in a newspaper.

Ad for the sale of used trucks:

Great selection of used vehicles. Save thousands in sale of trucks, prices below cost.

La gran selección de vehículos usados. Ahorre miles en la venta de camiones, precios a menos del costo.

Sale ends this weekend at El Toro Ford.

La venta termina este fin de semana en El Toro Ford.

Ad for the sale of furniture:

Get the lowest prices at the Alameda Furniture Store.

Obtenga los precios mínimos en muebles en la Alameda Furniture Store.

Nothing down, 1.9% interest rate, no payments until next January.

Nada de enganche, uno punto nueve porcentaje de interés, ningún pago hasta el siguiente enero.

Ad for pet grooming service:

We treat your pet like royalty.

Tratamos a su mascota como realeza.

Let us pamper your puppy for just $49.95.

Déjenos mimar a su perrito por solo cuarenta y nueve dólares con noventa y cinco centavos.

Come see us at 100 Solano.

Venga a vernos en la calle Solano, numero cien.

Advertising on the Radio

If you listen to any English-speaking radio station you will find that there is very little, if any, advertising aimed at Hispanics. Music is universal and there are many Hispanics, especially young ones, who listen to music with English lyrics. An advertisement here and there, in Spanish, would definitely produce results. Included below are phrases that you may find in radio advertisements.

Go to audio file 12g
Advertising on the radio.

The following are general phrases that can be used in advertising by a grocery store and a service provider:

Come shop at our store.	Venga a comprar en nuestra tienda.
We have the best prices.	Tenemos los mejores precios.
You do not have to wait in line.	Usted no tiene que esperar en línea.
We will cash your check.	Haremos efectivo su cheque.
We accept food subsidy stamps.	Aceptamos estampillas del subsidio de comida.
We are open 24 hours.	Estamos abiertos veinticuatro horas.
No repair is too large or too small.	Ninguna reparación es demasiada grande o demasiada pequeña.
We will provide you a free estimate.	Le proveeremos una estimación gratis.
Our workers are certified.	Nuestros trabajadores están certificados.
We are prompt and courteous.	Somos prestos y corteses.
We guarantee our work.	Garantizamos nuestro trabajo.

The following sentences could be used to encourage people to register to vote:

Have you registered to vote?	¿Se ha registrado usted para votar?
It is your right and responsibility to vote.	Es su derecho y su responsabilidad votar.
Your vote can make a difference.	Su voto puede hacer una diferencia.
Go to the county office at 100 Loma Street and register today.	Vaya a la oficina del condado en la calle Loma, número cien y regístrese hoy.

Television Advertising

Television is probably the medium that reaches the most people. It is also undoubtedly the most expensive form of advertising. Television stations are beginning to increase the number of programs broadcast in Spanish. Spanish TV programming provides an exceptional opportunity for businesses to reach out to the Hispanic customer. We will not attempt to provide any translated text on television advertising. We believe that this process is very complex and requires professional people to develop the ad copy. We encourage businesses to use people fluent in Spanish to present their ads on television.

Creating an Internet "Presence"

The Internet provides an exceptional way for you to sell your products or services to a worldwide market. You can reach that market almost instantaneously by developing a website. Technically, your website is an ad in cyberspace. Included in this section are a few samples of what you can include on your website to sell your own or someone else's products and services.

How do you refer to the World Wide Web, or WWW in Spanish? Spanish has two translations for World Wide Web:

World Wide Web	*la Red Mundial*
World Wide Web	*la Red Mundial de Comunicación*

It is perfectly acceptable and a lot easier to call it:

The web	*el web*

> Go to audio file 12h
> Advertising on the Internet.

If you have your own web-design business, you can use the following sentences to help market that business to Spanish-speaking customers:

Do you have a product you wish to sell on the Internet?	*¿Tiene un producto que desea vender en la Internet?*
Do you provide a service you wish to advertise on the Internet?	*¿Provee un servicio que desea anunciar en la Internet?*
We can help you.	*Le podemos ayudar.*
Let us design your website.	*Déjenos diseñar su sitio Web.*
We will design and submit it to search engines for less than $200.	*Lo diseñamos y lo sometemos a motores de búsqueda por menos de doscientos dólares.*
We guarantee that you will get inquiries within five days.	*Garantizamos que usted obtendrá búsquedas dentro de cinco días.*
Email us at…	*Envíenos un email a…*

You also might market products online. The following examples show sentences that would be useful for marketing printer cartridges online:

Need a cartridge for your printer?	*¿Necesita un cartucho para su impresora?*
Do you want to save money on printer cartridges?	*¿Quiere ahorrar dinero en cartuchos de la impresora?*
Save up to 60% on printer cartridges.	*Ahorre hasta sesenta porciento en cartuchos de la impresora.*
Click here to see a cartridge and price list.	*Haga clic aquí para ver una lista de cartuchos y precios.*

Summary

In this chapter we discussed how the business world does business with the Hispanic population. We showed that it is smart for businesses to try to talk to Hispanics in their native language. We provided material that can be used to sell cars, real estate, and investment instruments to Hispanics. We also cited some of the services offered by the legal profession. We provided translation with audio that law offices could use to advertise their services. Finally, we provided the translation of ads that can be placed in the newspaper, radio, and on a website to help reach Spanish-speaking readers and customers.

In the next chapter we will talk a little bit about the political world. We will concentrate on describing how our government operates under the constitution. We will provide a brief overview on the different levels of government, from the federal down to the local government office. We will also discuss what our rights and responsibilities are within our form of government.

Audio Files

13

The Political World

This chapter may seem like a lesson in civics. We will be discussing the Constitution and the Bill of Rights, and how they affect the lives of those living in the United States. This chapter also discusses the three branches of government that are prescribed by the Constitution for maintaining the balance of power, and how the provisions of the Constitution are implemented to govern at the federal, state, and local levels. We will end the chapter with a discussion of the rights and responsibilities of American citizens.

The intent of the material presented in this chapter is to provide translation that can be used to discuss the U.S. Constitution and form of government with a Hispanic. The chapter also presents translations of sentences that can be used to explain the process of obtaining U.S. citizenship, and the rights and responsibilities that accompany it.

In this chapter:

- ✳ Describing the U.S. Constitution
- ✳ Discussing the branches of government
- ✳ Reviewing our relationship with the government

United States Constitution

The U.S. Constitution is a complex document with a very simple mission, to protect the rights and freedom of the American people.

Go to audio file 13a The Constitution.

Many Hispanics risk their lives to enter the U.S. Those who have lived in the U.S. for a number of years are sometimes given the opportunity to apply for citizenship. The following discussion includes a couple of very simple questions a Hispanic might ask about the process of obtaining citizenship:

What do I have to do to become a U.S. citizen?	*¿Qué tengo que hacer para hacerme un ciudadano de los Estados Unidos?*
You must have a green card to prove residence in the U.S.	*Usted debe tener una tarjeta verde para probar residencia en los EEUU.*
Learn to read, write, speak, and understand English.	*Aprenda a leer, escribir, hablar, y entender el inglés.*
Study U.S. history and government.	*Estudie la historia y el gobierno de los EEUU.*
Apply for citizenship at the U.S. Citizen and Immigration Service office.	*Solicite ciudadanía en la Oficina de Servicios de Ciudadanía e Inmigración de los Estados Unidos.*

OBTAINING U.S. CITIZENSHIP

The citizenship application process is quite detailed and complex. The information offered here is just a simple overview of that process, and isn't meant to be legal advice. For detailed information, go to the website for the U.S. Citizenship and Immigration Services at http://uscis.gov/graphics/index.htm. USCIS offices are located in most cities in the U.S.

Here are some requirements to apply for citizenship:

* You must have lived in the U.S. as a lawful permanent resident (LPR) for five years (in other words, you must have a green card).

* You must have been physically present in the U.S. for 50% of those 5 years.

* You must not have spent more than 1 year outside the U.S.

* You must be at least 18 years old.

* You must have good moral character, no criminal conviction, have paid taxes, and registered for the draft (male).

* You must swear loyalty to the U.S. and its Constitution.

To apply, you must submit Form N-400 along with proof of lawful permanent residency (copy of both sides of the green card), to the local U.S. Citizenship and Immigration Services (USCIS) office. You will be tested at the USCIS office on your ability to speak English and your knowledge of U.S. history and government.

What happens after that?	*¿Qué ocurre después?*
You take a test on U.S. history and government.	*Usted toma un examen en la historia de los Estados Unidos y el gobierno.*
You have to demonstrate you can read, write, speak, and understand English.	*Usted tiene que demostrar que usted puede leer, escribir, hablar, y entender el inglés.*
You have to understand how the Constitution organized the government.	*Usted tiene que entender como organizó la Constitución el gobierno.*
What happens after the test?	*¿Qué ocurre después del examen?*
You have to take the oath of allegiance, and swear that you will support the Constitution.	*Usted tiene que tomar el juramento de lealtad y jurar que usted dará apoyo a la Constitución.*

What do you call an American or Americans from the U.S. in Spanish?

They are often called:

American	*los americanos*

A female and more than one Americans would be referred to as *la americana* and *los americanos*.

The term American, however, can refer to anyone from the American continent or North America and South America. Central America is considered part of North America. Hispanics refer to Americans from the U.S. as

American (male)	*el estadounidense*
American (female)	*la estadounidense*
Americans	*los estadounidenses*

Estadounidense is a literal translation of the phrase "from the United States."

Branches of Government

The U.S. Constitution provides that the government will be divided into three branches: the executive branch, the legislative branch, and the judicial branch. This allows for a system of checks and balances among the three branches.

Go to audio file 13b Branches of government.

A Hispanic who wishes to become a U.S. citizen may ask the following questions:

What does the Constitution say about the government?	*¿Qué dice la Constitución acerca del gobierno?*
The Constitution prescribes how the government is structured.	*La Constitución prescribe como el gobierno debe ser establecido.*
The federal government has three branches.	*El gobierno federal tiene tres ramas.*
The executive branch consists of the president and his cabinet.	*La rama ejecutiva consta del presidente y su gabinete.*
Congress is the Legislative Branch.	*El Congreso es la rama legislativa.*
Congress is made up of the House of Representatives and the Senate.	*El Congreso se compone de la Cámara de Representantes y el Senado.*
The judicial branch consists of the Supreme Court, and the federal and district courts.	*La rama judicial consta de la Corte Suprema, los tribunales federales y los tribunales de distrito.*
Why the three branches?	*¿Por qué las tres ramas?*
To provide checks and balances, so one branch doesn't dominate the others.	*Para proveer un mecanismo de equilibrio de poderes, para que una rama no domine a las demás.*
If two of the branches have an issue, the third branch will resolve the issue.	*Si dos de las ramas tienen un asunto, entonces la tercera rama resolverá el asunto.*

Federal Government

The three branches of government form the core of the federal government. The federalist framers of the Constitution wanted to ensure that the federal government had full power, and the states limited power, to govern our country. The executive branch, with all its departments, forms the biggest part of the federal government.

The following discussion will help a Hispanic learn more about the federal government:

Go to audio file 13c Federal government.

The Department of Homeland Security may be of most interest to a Hispanic seeking U.S. citizenship. It has jurisdiction over citizenship and immigration services.

What is the federal government?	¿Qué es el gobierno federal?
The federal government is the supreme law of the land.	El gobierno federal es la ley suprema del país.
The legislative branch, or Congress makes the laws.	La rama legislativa, o el Congreso hace las leyes.
The executive branch implements the laws.	La rama ejecutiva pone en práctica las leyes.
The judicial branch interprets the laws.	La rama judicial interpreta las leyes.
The executive branch includes departments that manage the nation's:	La rama ejecutiva incluye los departamentos que manejan para la nación:
security	la seguridad
defense	la defensa
health	la salud
energy	la energía
education	la educación
Who will decide if I can become a U.S. citizen?	¿Quién decidirá si puedo llegar a ser un ciudadano de los Estados Unidos?
The Immigration Service, under the Department of Homeland Security, will determine your eligibility to become a U.S. citizen.	El Servicio de Inmigración, bajo del Departamento de Seguridad Nacional, determinará su elegibilidad para convertirse en un ciudadano de los Estados Unidos.

FEDERAL GOVERNMENT OFFICES

The Spanish names for some of the U.S. federal government offices are shown here. For a complete list of government offices, including state offices, in Spanish go to http://www.firstgov.gov/Espanol/index.shtml.

Bureau of Citizenship and Immigration Services (BCIS)	La Oficina de Ciudadanía y Servicios Inmigratorios

(BCIS replaced the Immigration and Naturalization Service, or INS, under Homeland Security)

Department of Homeland Security	El Departamento de Seguridad Nacional
Department of Health and Human Services	El Departamento de Salud y Servicios Humanos

Department of Education	*El Departamento de Educación*
Department of Defense	*El Departamento de Defensa*
Social Security Administration	*La Administración del Seguro Social*

State Government

State government has the power to run the business of the respective state. It must operate under federal law. It has no authority or power over the federal government. State government can generate revenue to fund its needs by imposing income and sales taxes. A Hispanic person may be interested in how the state government will affect his or her life. The following sentences help to explain the role of state government:

Go to audio file 13d State government.

How will the state government affect my life if I become a resident of a state?	*¿Cómo afectará el gobierno del estado mi vida si me hago residente de un estado?*
Find out what the state law allows you to do and not do.	*Entérese en lo que la ley estatal le permite hacer y no hacer.*
You will have to pay taxes on your earnings in most states.	*Usted tendrá que pagar impuestos en sus ganancias en la mayoría de los estados.*
You must get a vehicle driver's license to drive.	*Usted debe obtener una licencia para manejar el vehículo.*
To get the license you must pass a written test, and demonstrate the ability to drive.	*Para obtener la licencia usted debe pasar una prueba escrita, y debe demostrar la habilidad para manejar.*
The state provides some social assistance to families.	*El estado provee alguna asistencia social para las familias.*
Your children will be eligible to attend in-state universities.	*Sus niños serán elegibles para asistir universidades dentro del estado de residencia.*

Local Government

This level of government has no direct power granted by the U.S. Constitution, but it probably has the most impact on our lives. The county and city tell us when we can water our lawn (in areas

Go to audio file 13e Local government.

where drought is a problem), where our children can or cannot skateboard, and how fast we drive. To top it off, they can tax our property and our food and medicine purchases.

A Hispanic may be interested in knowing what to expect from the local government when he or she moves his family into a local community. These sentences help to explain the functions of local government:

What can I expect from the local government?	¿Qué puedo esperar del gobierno local?
It will provide you water, gas, and sewage utility services.	Le proveerá el agua, el gas, y los servicios de utilidad de aguas residuales.
It will provide you police, ambulance, and fire protection services.	Le proveerá los servicios de policía, ambulancia, y de protección de fuego.
You have to obey the city's noise ordinances.	Usted tiene que obedecer las ordenanzas de ruido de la ciudad.
The city strictly enforces speed limits.	La ciudad estrictamente hace cumplir los límites de velocidad.
You must check with the city or county governments before you build a structure or wall on your property.	Usted debe consultar los gobiernos de la ciudad o del condado antes de que usted construya una estructura, o pared en su propiedad.
You have to ensure that your house and yard are well-maintained.	Usted tiene que asegurar que su casa y su patio estén bien mantenidos.

The Government and its Citizens

We take our freedom for granted, and oftentimes do not appreciate it. There are countless people living in oppression in countries that have no regard for individuals' freedom. Others live in countries that do not provide the opportunities to make a decent living. Many of them would love to live in a country like ours and enjoy the freedom and opportunities it provides. In this section, you learn terms and sentences that will be useful whenever you discuss the rights and responsibilities of U.S. citizenship with a Spanish-speaking individual.

Speaking About Your Rights as a U.S. Citizen

The Declaration of Independence states that all are "endowed by their Creator with certain unalienable Rights, that among these are Life,

Go to audio file 13f My rights.

Liberty and the pursuit of Happiness." American citizens have the right to enjoy their freedom without impediment by anyone or any government entity as long as they are not violating the law, or encroaching on someone else's freedom. A recently naturalized Hispanic might be interested in knowing what his or her rights are as a citizen of the U.S. The following sentences discuss those rights:

What are my rights as a citizen of this great country?	*¿Qué son mis derechos como un ciudadano de este gran país?*
You have the right to vote.	*Usted tiene el derecho de votar.*
You have the right to be treated equally by the government without regard to age, sex, race, or religion.	*Usted tiene el derecho de ser tratado igualmente por el gobierno sin hacer caso de la edad, el sexo, la raza, o la religión.*
You are covered by the Bill of Rights.	*Usted está protegido por la Declaración de los Derechos.*
What is the Bill of Rights?	*¿Qué es la Declaración de los Derechos?*
The Bill of Rights amended the U.S. Constitution.	*La Declaración de los Derechos enmendó la Constitución de los EEUU.*
The Bill of Rights guarantees:	*La Declaración de los Derechos garantiza:*
freedom of speech.	*la libertad de expresión.*
freedom of the press.	*la libertad de prensa.*
freedom to assemble.	*la libertad para congregarse.*
freedom of religion.	*la libertad de religión.*
protection against unreasonable searches and seizures.	*la protección en contra de las búsquedas irrazonables y los embargos.*
the right to keep and bear arms.	*el derecho para mantener y portar armas.*

The Preamble explains the purpose of the Constitution. The Preamble is included in the audio file that accompanies this section of the chapter (see the nearby sidebar for a full translation). Hispanics should be encouraged to learn the English version.

Go to audio file 13g The Preamble.

THE PREAMBLE OR EL PREÁMBULO

The Preamble to the Constitution of the United States of America is a clear and complete description of the Constitution's purpose. This short but eloquent text firmly establishes the Constitution's roots in the interests of peace, freedom, and equality for citizens of the United States. Here, the Preamble is presented in its original text and in Spanish translation.

THE PREAMBLE

We the People of the United States, in Order to form a more perfect Union, establish Justice, insure domestic Tranquility, provide for the common defence, promote the general Welfare, and secure the Blessings of Liberty to ourselves and our Posterity, do ordain and establish this Constitution for the United States of America.

EL PREÁMBULO

Nosotros el Pueblo de los Estados Unidos, a fin de formar una Unión más perfecta, establecer Justicia, afirmar Tranquilidad doméstica, proveer para la defensa común, promover el Bienestar general, y asegurar las Bendiciones de Libertad para nosotros mismos y nuestra Posteridad, ordenamos y establecemos esta Constitución para los Estados Unidos de América.

Discussing Your Responsibilities as a Citizen

There is no right without a corresponding responsibility.

As responsible citizens, we need to vote, live within the law, and do all we can to make sure that the freedoms we enjoy are not lost. Many have paid with their lives so we could have this freedom. Anyone who is about to become a citizen must be willing to accept the responsibility that comes with the rights of citizenship. A Hispanic that has just obtained citizenship might express the following:

Go to audio file 13h My responsibilities.

Listen Up

G

I am so happy with all the benefits of being a U.S. citizen.	Soy tan feliz con todos los beneficios de ser un ciudadano de los Estados Unidos.
Is there anything else I should know or do?	¿Hay cualquier otra cosa que debería saber o hacer?
You should register to vote.	Usted debería registrarse para votar.
When can I vote?	¿Cuándo puedo votar?
You can vote in national, state, and local elections.	Usted puede votar en elecciones nacionales, estatales, y locales.
You can vote in the next election if you register:	Usted puede votar en la siguiente elección si usted se registra:
by mail 30 days before the election.	por correo treinta días antes de la elección.
in person at the local or county office 15 days before the election.	en persona en la oficina local o del condado quince Días antes de la elección.
There are responsibilities that come with your rights as a citizen.	Hay responsabilidades que vienen con sus derechos como un ciudadano.
You should be a responsible citizen and comply with all local, state, and national laws.	Usted debería ser un ciudadano responsable y debería cumplir con todas las leyes locales, estatales, y nacionales.
Your allegiance should be to the U.S.	Su lealtad debería ser para los EEUU.
You must treat others equally without regard to age, sex, race, or religion.	Usted debe tratar por igual a los otros sin hacer caso de la edad, el sexo, la raza, o la religión.
You must respect other people's rights to free speech and to worship as they please.	Usted debe respetar los derechos ajenos para el discurso en libertad y para adorar como ellos quieran.

Summary

This chapter presented an overview of the political world. Any mention of politics brings up thoughts of all the mud slinging that takes place during an election year. In this chapter we talked about the good things that the federal, state, and local governments do for their citizens. We described how the Constitution established a federal government with executive, legislative, and judicial branches. We then described the rights and corresponding responsibilities we as citizens have.

In the final chapter we are going to provide three lists of words, phrases, and sentences that you will find helpful whenever you engage in conversations in Spanish. The information you learn in Chapter 14 covers a wide range of common terms and expressions not covered in previous chapters in this book.

Audio Files

Must-Know Words, Phrases, and Sentences

This, the final chapter of Speak Basic Spanish In No Time, provides words and phrases that can be very useful in a variety of situations. Though determining what counts as "must know" information can be a subjective process, we have attempted to include material in this chapter that we thought would be of the most help and interest to you. This chapter includes phrases that can be used to request assistance in one of several emergency situations. It also includes a detailed description of the interrogative words, such as where, what, when, and so on. These same English words can be used in non-interrogative phrases, so this chapter explains how you can tell whether a word is interrogative or non-interrogative. We conclude the chapter with phrases that use adverbs to describe frequency, words that serve as links between ideas, and a few rejoinders.

14

In this chapter:

* Getting help in an emergency situation
* Learning about the interrogatives
* Describing words that identify frequency, provide links, or offer rejoinders

Words and Phrases for Emergencies

The following phrases can be used to request help in a variety of emergency situations. They can be used to request assistance using the telephone or by calling out to some passerby.

Go to audio file 14a Calling for help.

Help!	*¡Auxilio!*
Help me.	*¡Ayúdame!*
Please help me.	*Por favor ayúdame.*
I need help.	*Necesito ayuda.*
I have an emergency.	*Tengo una emergencia.*
Someone please help me!	*¡Alguien por favor ayúdame!*
My house is on fire.	*Mi casa está ardiendo.*
Someone broke into my house.	*Alguien forzó la entrada en mi casa.*
I have been robbed.	*He sido robado.*
I have been assaulted.	*He sido asaltada.*
My car is on fire.	*Mi coche está ardiendo.*
My wife fell down.	*Mi esposa se cayó.*
My wife had a stroke.	*Mi esposa tuvo una apoplejía.*
My husband fainted.	*Mi esposo se desmayó.*
I am having chest pain.	*Estoy teniendo dolor del pecho.*
I need nitroglycerin.	*Necesito nitroglicerina.*
The nitroglycerin is in my pocket.	*La nitroglicerina está en mi bolsillo.*
Put one pill under my tongue.	*Pon una píldora bajo mi lengua.*
Spray two doses under my tongue.	*Rocía dos dosis bajo mi lengua.*
Take me to the hospital.	*Llévame al hospital.*
Please call an ambulance.	*Por favor llama una ambulancia.*
Please call the police.	*Por favor llama a la policía.*
Please call 911!	*¡Por favor llama al nueve uno uno!*

Using Spanish Terms for Where, When, Who and Other Interrogatives

In this section we introduce you to Spanish translations for words used to ask questions. Called interrogatives, some of these terms are pronouns, such as what, who, and which. Others are descriptive interrogatives, such as the terms when, where, why and how. In Spanish the interrogative words are qué, quién, cuál, cuándo, dónde, por qué, and cómo. The Spanish interrogative always has an accent.

Many of the interrogatives can also be used in non-interrogative statements. In those cases, they generally do not have an accent, as shown in the underscored *que* in this example:

That is what is needed.   *Eso es lo que se necesita.*

In this chapter, English words are listed followed by translated interrogative phrases. Some non-interrogative phrases will also be shown.

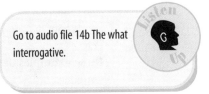

note There are exceptions to the rule on accenting exclamation phrases, as you learn later in the section titled "Using 'How.'"

Go to audio file 14b The what interrogative.

Using "What"

The Spanish translation for what, as used to refer to ideas or things, is qué. In these examples, "what" is used as an interrogative:

What?	*¿Qué?*
What can I do?	*¿Qué puedo hacer?*
What can I do for you?	*¿Qué puedo hacer para ti?*
What do you say?	*¿Qué te parece?*
What does it matter to me?	*¿A mí qué?*
What else?	*¿Qué más?*
What for?	*¿Para qué?*
What happened?	*¿Qué pasó?*
What's new?	*¿Qué hay de nuevo?*
What's on your mind?	*¿En qué estás pensando?*
What's the matter?	*¿Qué ocurre?*

The word que does not have an accent in the non-interrogative form, as shown in these examples:

I know that I can learn to speak Spanish.	Sé que puedo aprender a hablar español.
I am positive that I will succeed.	Estoy positivo que tendré éxito.
The car that I bought is a classic.	El coche que compré es un clásico.
She is taller than him.	Ella es más alta que él.

Using "Who" and "Whom"

Here are examples of sentences that ask questions using the words "who" and "whom":

Go to audio file 14c The who and which interrogatives.

Who?	¿Quién?
Who is this gift for?	¿Para quién es este regalo?
Who lives here?	¿Quién vive aquí?
Whom did you invite?	¿A quiénes invitaste?

These examples demonstrate the use of "who" and "whom" in non-interrogative sentences:

It does not matter who is here.	No importa quien esté aquí.
Those whom I invited brought gifts.	Aquéllos a quienes invité trajeron regalos.

LEARNING SPANISH BY READING A SPANISH NEWSPAPER

Reading Spanish newspapers is an excellent way to improve your understanding of the Spanish language. The following link provides access to several online English/Spanish newspapers from the U.S. and Latin American countries for reading practice:

http://www.englishspanishlink.com/peoples%20news.htm

This site is an excellent tool for learning Spanish. It links to newspapers including the *Wall Street Journal, La Raza,* and *El Nuevo Herald* published in the U.S. The site is bilingual. It provides an online Toolbox that has several dictionaries, a grammar guide, a translator, and other tools to help you learn Spanish. It includes many phrases in English and Spanish. Practice reading a Spanish newspaper after you have read or heard the news in English.

Using "Which"

The word "which," or *cuál*, is used to select between things. *Cuál* has a plural form. The following adjective interrogatives illustrate the use of the word *cuál*:

Which is the car that you like?	¿Cuál es el coche que te gusta?
Which of these cars do you want?	¿Cuál de estos coches quieres tú?

In this example, "which" is used in a non-interrogative sentence:

The car which I bought 3 years ago still looks good.	El coche el cual compré tres años atrás todavía luce bien.

Using "When"

These examples demonstrate the use of "when" as an interrogative:

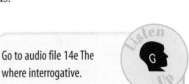

Go to audio file 14d The when interrogative.

When?	¿Cuándo?
When can you do it?	¿Cuándo lo puedes hacer?
When can we get together?	¿Cuándo podemos juntarnos?
When can we go to dinner?	¿Cuándo podemos ir a cenar?
When did it happen?	¿Cuándo ocurrió?
When do you arrive?	¿Cuándo llegas?
When do you leave?	¿Cuándo sales?

The following examples demonstrate the use of "when" in statements:

Call me when you arrive.	Llámame cuando llegues.
I'll call you when I arrive.	Te llamaré cuando llegue.
I'll do it when I can.	Lo haré cuando pueda.
Do it when you can.	Hazlo cuando puedas.

Using "Where"

Go to audio file 14e The where interrogative.

These examples demonstrate the use of "where" as an interrogative:

Where?	¿Dónde?
Where is the key?	¿Dónde está la llave?
Where is the phone?	¿Dónde está el teléfono?
Where is the street?	¿Dónde está la calle?

Where are the keys?	*¿Dónde están las llaves?*
Where are the children?	*¿Dónde están los niños?*
Where are you?	*¿Dónde estás tú?*
Where were you last night?	*¿Dónde estuviste anoche?*
Where do you live?	*¿Dónde vives?*
Where have you been?	*¿Dónde has estado?*

Note how the Spanish word *dónde* changes when the "to where" form is used, as in this example:

Where are you going?	*¿Adónde vas?*

The following shows the translation for the "from where" form of this phrase:

Where are you coming from?	*¿De dónde vienes?*
Where are you from?	*¿De dónde eres?*

In these examples, "where" is used as a non-interrogative:

It rained where I live.	*Llovió donde vivo.*
I don't know where I left it.	*No sé donde lo dejé.*
Where there is life there is hope.	*Donde hay vida hay esperanza.*
Where there is smoke there is fire.	*Donde hay humo hay fuego.*

Using "Why"

In the first group of interrogative phrase transla-tions, you learned that the Spanish word for "what" is *qué*. This word is also used in the trans-lation of the word "why."

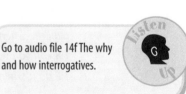

Go to audio file 14f The why and how interrogatives.

Why?	*¿Por qué?*
Why did you do it?	*¿Por qué lo hiciste?*
Why not?	*¿Por qué no?*
Why didn't you do it?	*¿Por qué no lo hiciste?*

The response to these questions is usually *porque* (because) followed by a statement that explains "why." The *que* is unaccented. The following responses match the pre-ceding questions:

Because it is important.	*Porque es importante.*
Because I wanted to.	*Porque quise.*
Because it is not good for you.	*Porque no es bueno para ti.*
Because I did not want to.	*Porque no quise.*

If the phrase *por qué*, or "why" in Spanish, is included in the non-interrogative form, it will have an accent on the *qué*, as shown in the following two phrases:

I don't know why he did it.	*No sé por qué él lo hizo.*
It is not for me to reason why.	*No es para que yo razone por qué.*

Using "How"

The word "how" can be used to ask in what way something happened. Here are some examples of sentences using the term "how" as an interrogative:

How?	*¿Cómo?*
How are you?	*¿Cómo estás?*
How did you get here?	*¿Cómo viniste tú?*
How are you going to pay for it?	*¿Cómo vas a pagarlo?*

In these examples, "how" is used in statements, rather than questions:

Show me how you did it.	*Muéstrame como lo hiciste.*
I will show you how to do it.	*Te mostraré como hacerlo.*

Interrogative words in exclamation phrases are accented even if the phrase is not interrogative, and therefore does not end in a question mark. The punctuation on these phrases is an exclamation mark. The following examples illustrate this exception to the rule on accents:

How beautiful!	*¡Qué bonito!*
How exciting!	*¡Qué emocionante!*
How extraordinary!	*¡Qué extraordinario!*
How frightening!	*¡Qué susto!*
How kind of you!	*¡Qué amabilidad la suya!*
How wonderful it is!	*¡Qué bien está!*
How interesting!	*¡Qué interesante!*
What a blessing!	*¡Qué bendición!*
What a coincidence!	*¡Qué coincidencia!*
What a life!	*¡Qué vida!*
What a relief!	*¡Qué alivio!*
What a shame!	*¡Qué lástima!*
What a shock!	*¡Qué susto!*
What a surprise!	*¡Qué sorpresa!*

Using Frequency Adverbs (You'll Always Be Glad You Know These Terms)

Go to audio file 14g Words that describe frequency, links, and rejoinders.

Frequency adverbs, such as "never" and "always," describe how often things happen. In this section, you see the same basic sentence altered by the use of various frequency adverbs. The adverbs are underscored in the Spanish translated phrases so you can identify them.

She always calls.	Ella _siempre_ llama.
She usually calls.	Ella llama _normalmente_.
She often calls.	Ella llama _a menudo_.
She sometimes calls.	Ella llama _algunas veces_.
She seldom calls.	Ella llama _pocas veces_.
She rarely calls.	Ella llama _muy pocas veces_.
She never calls.	Ella _nunca_ llama.

Words That Link Phrases

There are certain words that provide a link between ideas, or phrases and individual words. Some of these words are

for example	por ejemplo
whatever	lo que sea
moreover, furthermore, or besides	además
yet	aún
therefore	por lo tanto
then	entonces
meanwhile	entretanto
that is	o sea
at any rate	sea como sea
ever since	desde entonces
once	una vez
always	siempre
never	nunca
still	todavía
sometimes	a veces
almost	casi
not only, but also	no solamente, sino que también

Using Common Rejoinders

The last thing we would like include in this chapter is a series of rejoinders. These are little phrases that you use to keep the conversation going, or to show that you are interested in what is being discussed.

Really?	¿De veras?
No way!	¡De ninguna manera!
Excellent idea.	Ésa es una idea excelente.
I agree with you.	Estoy de acuerdo contigo.
Me too.	Yo también.
Don't tell me.	No me digas.
And you?	¿Y tú?
And you?	¿Y usted?
right?	¿verdad?

tip You can use the rejoinders you learn in this chapter even when you do not fully understand what is being said in Spanish.

Go to audio file 14h Slang.

A SPANISH CONVERSATION IN SLANG

Each Latin American country has its own set of slang words. The following conversation offers a sampling of some of this slang.

Hey man! What's happening?	¡Ese bato! ¿Qué te pasa?
You look like death paid you a visit.	Parece que te visitó la flaca.
Give me a break.	Pásame quebrada.
I studied hard, but my professor did not give me a break in Biology.	Me quemé las pestañas estudiando pero el profe no me pasó quebrada en la biología.
Did you challenge him?	¿Le hiciste mitote?
Yes, but he ignored me.	Sí, pero me tiró a Lucas.
I am tired of that class.	Estoy hasta el gorro con esa clase.
I did great in all my other classes.	Me aventé en todas las otras clases.
I am happy for one thing.	Una cosa me parece a todo dar.

| The professor sped away angrily in his old car when I complained. | El profe salió enchilado quemando llanta en su carcancha cuando le reclamé. |
| The police stopped him and gave him a ticket. I'm sure it cost him plenty of money. | Lo cachó la patrulla y le dio un tiquete. De seguro que le costó bastante lana. |

There is an excellent slang dictionary that includes slang from all Latin American countries at http://www.jergasdehablahispana.org/

Practicing Conversational Spanish

The following Spanish conversational dialogue includes text from all the chapters in this book. The chapter where the phrase or part of the phrase came from is shown on the right side. Try to read the phrase and reinforce your learning by listening to the audio file. If you have trouble

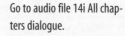
Go to audio file 14i All chapters dialogue.

translating any phrase in this dialogue, you can look up the translation in the applicable chapter.

A: Hola. Soy Julia. ¿Cómo te llamas?	(ch 3)
B: Me llamo Victor. ¿De dónde eres?	(ch 3)
A: Vivo en esta ciudad. Soy estadounidense. ¿Y tú?	(ch 3/13/14)
B: Vivo en Puerto Rico. ¿Estás casada?	(ch 3)
A: Soy soltera ¿Y tú?	(ch 3)
B: Estoy divorciado. Tengo dos hijos.	(ch 4)
A: ¿Qué edades tienen?	(ch 4)
B: Ocho y seis. Van a una escuela primaria.	(ch 2/4)
A: ¡Excelente!	(ch 14)
B: ¿Dónde vives?	(ch 5)
A: Vivo en un apartamento cerca del supermercado.	(ch 5)
B: No me digas. Compro abarrotes en el supermercado.	(ch 14/7)
A: Yo también. Compré comida para mi perro.	(ch 14/1)
A: ¿Hay cualquiera cosa que necesitas saber cerca de nuestra ciudad?	(ch 10)
B: Necesito más información sobre los restaurantes.	(ch 10)
B: Busco un restaurante que sirve comida hispana auténtica.	(ch 8)
A: Recomiendo el Restaurante de Mariscos.	(ch 8)
B: Gracias. Me gusta comer.	(ch 10/8)

A: ¿Cómo está tu salud?   (ch 9)

B: Estuve involucrado en un accidente del automóvil. Sufrí lesiones
de la espalda.   (ch 12)

A: Lo siento. ¿Qué hora es?   (ch 8/2)

B: Son las dos y media de la tarde.   (ch 2)

A: ¿Qué vas a hacer después del trabajo?   (ch 6)

B: Voy a ir a la oficina del dentista, ¿Y tú?   (ch 6/14)

A: Voy a ir de paseo en la calma de la tarde.   (ch 11)

B: ¡Qué vida!   (ch 14)

BOOSTING YOUR CONVERSATIONAL SKILLS

Anytime you need a refresher in the basics of conversational Spanish, you can refer back to a few key chapters in this book.

As you practice your conversational Spanish, refer frequently to the sections titled "Breaking the Ice" and "Basic Greetings" in Chapter 3. Those two sections provide the highest number of repetitions of the same phrases. The repetitions teach you all options in the formal/informal form of address and how gender affects the basic greeting phrases.

You will also benefit from periodically reviewing Chapter 1, "The Rules--Short and Sweet." That chapter will help you understand what makes the same letters sound so different when used in the English and Spanish languages. That chapter also explains the special characters used to stress syllables in words, and how certain letter combinations expand on the sounds created by the letters in the alphabet.

As you become more comfortable and familiar with the material presented in these and other chapters of this book, you will develop communication skills that many people would love to have.

Summary and Conclusion

This chapter included a potpourri of Spanish terms that you'll use often when speaking to your Spanish friends and co-workers. Here, you learned words and phrases that you can use to call for help in an emergency situation. The chapter also offered a detailed description of the Spanish interrogative words, and how they are used and accented, along with a large number of translated phrases using those words. It also explained how the same Spanish words can be used in non-interrogative phrases. The chapter also covered the use of frequency adverbs, and concluded with the translation of a short list of rejoinders.

Speak Basic Spanish In No Time has provided you with brief, easy-to-understand, written instruction on how to learn to understand written and spoken Spanish. This book hasn't emphasized rote memorization of grammar rules; instead, its goal has been to encourage you to listen and learn the material presented in the easily accessible audio files. By reviewing the written material and audio provided in this book, you will develop the ability to not only understand, but also participate in conversations in Spanish.

You are not the same person you were before you read *Speak Basic Spanish In No Time*, and listened to the audio files it provides. Even if you only skimmed through the book, and listened to selected audio files that you were interested in, you now have more capability than you did before you began reading this book. With the skills you've learned here, you will no longer feel totally lost when you hear someone speak Spanish. When a friend, co-worker, or business owner speaks Spanish, you'll be able to understand at least some of the words you hear.

So, the next time you see a Hispanic person, don't think of him or her as a foreigner. Think of that person as someone who is as interested in learning from you as you are in learning from him or her. Smile, and strike up a conversation!

Part IV

Appendix

References and Resources

This appendix lists resources that are readily available, and that we can recommend as useful tools for improving your Spanish-language skills. Where appropriate, the listings include short reviews or additional descriptions to explain the kind and quality of information provided by the resource.

This list was current at the time of this writing, but be aware that availability and costs may change over time. You can use this list as a starting point, however, to help you in finding your own resources for learning and becoming fluent in Spanish.

Books on Learning Spanish

Title: *Búscalo (Look It Up!)*
Author: William B. Clarkson
Publisher: John Wiley & Sons Inc
ISBN: 0471245607
Format: Paperback
List Price: $ 15.95

This quick reference guide to Spanish grammar includes more than 500 entries that provide word definitions and explanations of how to use defined terms in a sentence. This book also provides a pronunciation guide.

Title: *Conversational Spanish in Nothing Flat*

Author: Mark Frobose

Publisher: Language Dynamics Inc.; (April 21, 2002)

ISBN: 1893564568

A 200 page book with eight one-hour CDs. Cost: $69

According to reviews on the Internet, this book is an exceptional tool for learning to speak Spanish. It uses a language dynamics concept that provides same page answer keys for faster access to answers to your questions.

Title: *Spanish for Gringos: Learn Spoken Spanish Without Taking a Course*

Author: William C. Harvey

Publisher: Barron's Educational Series, Incorporated

ISBN: 0764176781

Format: Paperback, 200pp

Pub. Date: September 2003

Edition Description: Book & three CDs

One of the lines in this book's ad is "Pick up the language without taking a course!" This book teaches you how to understand and speak very basic conversational Spanish without having to take a formal language course.

Learn Spanish Using Audio Systems

The Pimsleur Method allows you to learn a language without any reading materials. This course consists of a series of 30-minute audio sessions, which you can listen to at your own pace. You can get more information at http://www.languagetapes.com/whypimsleur.html#languagecoursefeatures

Title: *Listen and Learn Spanish*

ISBN: 0486999181

Format: Audio

Pub. Date: February 1991

Publisher: Dover Publications, Incorporated

This is one of the most efficient language learning courses ever designed for travelers. Each set contains 90 minutes of speech: English, then Spanish followed by a pause for repetition. Cassettes fit all standard players, including portables. Each set contains one cassette and manual.

Websites That Help You Learn Spanish

http://spanish.about.com/

This site is probably the best on the Internet for anyone trying to learn Spanish, especially Spanish grammar. It has clear and easy-to-understand lessons for beginners as well as advanced learners. It includes an extensive list of grammar terms, their definitions, and instruction on use. Clear and simple examples are provided in both English and Spanish. The site includes audio to help in the pronunciation of words. The site also includes features such as proverbs, sayings, descriptions of Latin American countries' cultures, and an extensive list of other learning resources.

http://www.spanish.bz/index.html

This site provides good tools for learning Spanish. It provides free, easy-to-understand lessons on Spanish grammar with audio. It also provides worksheets and quizzes that allow you to practice what you learned. This site includes beautiful video of the sights and a brief description of the culture of several Latin American countries.

http://www.studyspanish.com/vocab/

The *Study Spanish* website provides a free online tutorial. It includes the Spanish translation, including audio, of words related to a variety of topics.

http://www.wordreference.com/index.htm

At this site you will find one of the most complete English-to-Spanish and Spanish-to-English dictionaries on the Internet. It provides several translation forms of the word you enter.

Spanish Language Newspapers Online

You may be able to find local and regional news written in Spanish for your city and state online. If not, there are two exceptional websites where you will find Spanish-language regional, national, and international news. As you browse these sites, look for those articles on news that you have already heard in English. That will help you understand what you are attempting to read in Spanish. Yahoo! and CNN provide the websites.

http://espanol.news.yahoo.com/

http://cnnenespanol.com/

Spanish Language Television Programming

A good way to learn Spanish is to listen to the news in Spanish. Most cable and satellite dish television service includes channels that provide programming and the news in Spanish.

Because you have heard that news in English you will be better able to understand what is being reported in Spanish. It will take a while for you to learn what is being said, because Spanish newscasters have the tendency to talk a little bit too fast. Variety and soap opera shows, known as telenovelas, can be entertaining as well as educational. Two major providers of quality Spanish programs are Univisión and Galavisión.

Magazines en Español

Many popular English magazines are also published in Spanish. The Spanish publications include the same article and news format found in the English versions. These magazines include

> *People En Español*
>
> *Reader's Digest Selecciones—Spanish Edition*
>
> *National Geographic en Español*
>
> *Cosmopolitan en Español*
>
> *Men's Health en Español*
>
> *Estylo (Style)*

Reading these magazines is another great way to learn Spanish. The articles generally include plenty of pictures, which help novice Spanish-language readers translate and understand the text. These magazines can be purchased single copy or through subscription. You should be able to find some of these magazines at your supermarket or newsstand. If not, you can subscribe to any of them at the following website:

http://www.worldsearch.com/marketplace/books_and_media/magazines/spanish-language/

Index

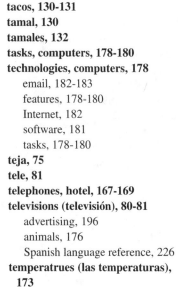

X - Y - Z

Index of Spanish Terms

Do Even More
...In No Time

Must See

Get ready to cross off those items on your to-do list! *In No Time* helps you tackle the projects that you don't think you have time to finish. With shopping lists and step-by-step instructions, these books get you working toward accomplishing your goals.

Check out these other *In No Time* books, coming soon!

Start Your Own Home Business In No Time
ISBN: **0-7897-3224-6**
$16.95
September 2004

Plan a Fabulous Party In No Time
ISBN: **0-7897-3221-1**
$16.95
September 2004

Organize Your Personal Fiances In No Time
ISBN: **0-7897-3179-7**
$16.95
August 2004

Organize Your Garage In No Time
ISBN: **0-7897-3219-X**
$16.95
October 2004

Quick Family Meals In No Time
ISBN: **0-7897-3299-8**
$16.95
October 2004

Organize Your Family's Schedule In No Time
ISBN: **0-7897-3220-3**
$16.95
October 2004